W9-BCF-376

edited by

HUGO A. BEDAU
Tufts University

JUSTICE AND EQUALITY

Prentice-Hall, Inc., Englewood Cliffs, New Jersey

Library of Congress Catalog Card Number: 76–140685

Printed in the United States of America

C 13–514133–8
P 13–514125–7

Current Printing (last digit):
10 9 8 7 6 5 4 3 2 1

PRENTICE-HALL INTERNATIONAL, INC., London
PRENTICE-HALL OF AUSTRALIA, PTY., LTD., Sydney
PRENTICE-HALL OF CANADA, LTD., Toronto
PRENTICE-HALL OF INDIA PRIVATE LIMITED, New Delhi
PRENTICE-HALL OF JAPAN, INC., Tokyo

CENTRAL ISSUES IN PHILOSOPHY SERIES

BARUCH A. BRODY
series editor

Baruch A. Brody
MORAL RULES AND PARTICULAR CIRCUMSTANCES

Hugo A. Bedau
JUSTICE AND EQUALITY

Mark Levensky
HUMAN FACTUAL KNOWLEDGE

George I. Mavrodes
THE RATIONALITY OF BELIEF IN GOD

Robert Sleigh
NECESSARY TRUTH

David M. Rosenthal
MATERIALISM AND THE MIND-BODY PROBLEM

Richard Grandy
THEORIES AND OBSERVATIONS IN SCIENCE

Gerald Dworkin
DETERMINISM, FREE WILL, AND MORAL RESPONSIBILITY

David P. Gauthier
MORALITY AND RATIONAL SELF-INTEREST

Charles Landesman
THE FOUNDATIONS OF KNOWLEDGE

Adrienne and Keith Lehrer
THEORY OF MEANING

Foreword

The Central Issues in Philosophy series is based upon the conviction that the best way to teach philosophy to introductory students is to experience or to *do* philosophy with them. The basic unit of philosophical investigation is the particular problem, and not the area or the historical figure. Therefore, this series consists of sets of readings organised around well-defined, manageable problems. All other things being equal, problems that are of interest and relevance to the students have been chosen.

Each volume contains an introduction that clearly defines the problem and sets out the alternative positions that have been taken. The selections are chosen and arranged in such a way as to take the student through the dialectic of the problem; each reading, besides presenting a particular point of view, criticizes the points of view set out earlier.

Although no attempt has been made to introduce the student in a systematic way to the history of philosophy, classical selections relevant to the development of the problem have been included. As a side benefit, the student will therefore come to see the continuity, as well as the breaks, between classical and contemporary thought. But in no case will a selection be included merely for its historical significance; clarity of expression and systematic significance are the main criteria for selection.

Baruch A. Brody

Contents

Introduction

History and current events show that we live in a world where few men receive their just deserts, mighty nations wage unjust war against their smaller neighbors, and the bounty of nature is unfairly distributed among the peoples of the earth. The chief social problems in our midst today—racism, poverty, and war—result in and are in large part the result of injustice, unfairness, and inequality.

It is as easy to render such sweeping criticism of our social institutions as it is difficult to reform them in order to remove these defects. Undoubtedly, part of the difficulty lies in our inability or unwillingness to obtain accurate factual description and causal explanation of men's conduct and of how our institutions really work. For example, what really are the social and psychological consequences of enforced school segregation; what are likely to be the consequences of enforced school desegregation; and what might the consequences be of alternatives to either of these methods of coping with racism in American society? Newspaper writers, social and behavioral scientists, and all sensitive observers have an enormous responsibility to diagnose our social ills and convince us of their causes and consequences so as to enable us to decide on sound remedies.

But an equally perplexing part of the difficulty in overcoming injustice is the seeming abstractness, instability, and variety of the ideals of justice. It may be true (so the complaint might run) that sociologists and others are needed to diagnose the sources of individual and institutional injustices, but it is philosophers who owe us an intelligible, sound criterion of justice. They have failed, however, as their endless sequence of incompatible theories on the subject all too plainly shows. When the reader has finished studying the essays in this volume he may not find this complaint especially plausible. But there is truth in its premise. It is definitely and characteristically a philosophical task to study social ideals, to assess their structure and justification, to lay bare the factual considerations which support (or undermine) them. No effective social criticism can proceed unless it is fully armed from this quarter.

Put in the briefest possible way, therefore, the chief issues for philosophical inquiry here are these: What is justice? What is equality? How are the two related? What facts about men and society must a theory of justice and equality take into account? It is the purpose of the selections collected in this volume to introduce the reader to these questions, to give him some perspective on how philosophers have pondered them, and to assist him in answering them, however tentatively, for himself. In the brief space available, it is impossible to provide the detail needed for final answers to be achieved. Nevertheless, the selections will show the full range of relevant questions and guarantee that the reader has confronted the central issues of traditional and contemporary interest.

This volume is divided, roughly, into two overlapping parts. The first set of essays begins with Aristotle's classic discussion of the entire range of problems, during which he presents his own meritarian theory of justice. This is followed by statements of the modern liberal and utilitarian conceptions of justice as developed by Hobbes, Hume, and J. S. Mill, and culminates with the contemporary classic, "Justice as Fairness," by John Rawls and the critique of this essay by Brian Barry. Rawls' essay is also the first of six taken from current philosophical debate which focuses upon the relation of justice and equality, the concept of just inequalities, and the ideal of equality. The essay by Bernard Williams investigates the idea and ideal of equality; J. R. Lucas attacks our "obsession" with equality; Stanley Benn responds to the attack. Together with the concluding essay by the editor, the second set of essays provides a broad appraisal of the current status and vicissitudes of egalitarianism.

The central issues of this volume are perennial ones, and each is posed in a different way by the four classic philosophers presented here. Accordingly, in the rest of this introduction, I shall concentrate mainly on the views of Aristotle, Hobbes, Hume, and Mill, with only occasional brief mention of the revision and extension their views receive at the hands of their successors in the remaining selections. A word of caution is in order. Although I review the selections in this volume roughly in their chronological order, there is little presumption in favor of studying them in that sequence. Much can be said for beginning not with Aristotle but with Mill, or Rawls, or Williams. There is no one way to study these theories of justice and equality, just as there is no one place to start from in order to construct one's own position on these matters.

Aristotle's essay on justice in Book V of his *Nichomachean Ethics* is undoubtedly the most influential single treatment ever written on the subject. Not even Plato's *Republic,* ten times as long and ostensibly designed to answer the question, "What is justice?" deserves priority. Plato's dialogue is so massively preoccupied with epistemological and metaphysical matters, which do little to advance our understanding of justice, that it often seems he has deliberately sacrificed the original topic to his other philosophical interests. Also, Plato's manifest topic, *dikaiosyne,* though usually translated as "justice," has a far wider meaning, with the result that even when Plato is discussing *dikaiosyne,* we learn less than we may think we do about justice. *Dikaiosyne* is more nearly what we mean by "rectitude," right conduct, whereas it is clear that for us, justice is not identifiable with right conduct. For example, the right thing to do in a situation might be to hold one's tongue, but it would not therefore be true or even make sense to say that speaking out would be unjust. Aristotle's discussion of justice does not suffer the fault of changing the subject in either of these ways.

Aristotle's examination of justice also has particular merits in the present collection by virtue of its pith and comprehensiveness and because Hobbes, Hume, and Mill can all be read as departures from his position. Aristotle not only offers us views on all the major issues in a theory of justice, he also helps to organize the field for subsequent investigation through development of a battery of permanently useful distinctions. He contrasts justice as the whole of virtue (roughly, Plato's *dikaiosyne*) with justice as a specific virtue; and within the latter he invites us to distinguish distributive justice (about which we are mainly concerned in this book) from rectificatory or remedial justice. We come to see the need for a distinction between justice as rule-governed conduct in conformity to law, and justice as corrective equity, designed to take into account special cases unforeseeable by even the wisest of law makers. In political justice he requires us to distinguish between "natural justice" (justice for all persons everywhere and everywhen), and "conventional justice" (justice according to the laws and usages of a given community). The latter introduces variations missing from the former. And we are brought to see the need to distinguish between a particular act of justice and its universal or defining principle, and to contrast both the justice of an act and justice itself with the justice in a man, a trait of character. On many of these topics the other selections provide no further discussion. All the more value, therefore, in having at the start one philosopher's view of the full range of issues raised which shape a theory of justice.

Despite the opportunities afforded by some two thousand years of study of Aristotle's views, scholars are by no means in agreement on a number of questions, with the result that beginning students are likely to want guidance in interpreting the text which cannot easily be provided them. Two such issues deserve to be mentioned here as they are among the more prominent and interesting. One concerns the nature of justice in economic relationships, an issue on which several other selections in this book also have a bearing. Aristotle, in Chapter 5, makes it reasonably clear that he thinks wages and prices are entirely governed by "demand" between the parties involved, and therefore in no way subject to any of his principles of distributive justice. But does it follow from this that Aristotle denies that there is such a concept as a "just wage" or a "fair price;" or is it only that on his views as they stand we have no way of interpreting these concepts? Another vexed matter, one peculiar to Aristotle's theory, is his famous doctrine (also in Chapter 5) that justice, like all virtues, is a "mean" between extremes of vice. We can see the idea he has in mind plainly enough if we think of a person seeking compensation (remedial justice) for some injury suffered at the hands of another. Aristotle would argue that the injured party should not seek too much (for that would be an unfair gain at the other's expense) nor too little (for that would impose on himself an unfair loss). Seen in this way, the notion that justice is a mean between extremes of vice seems true enough, but unfortunately rather trivial and unhelpful. For we are not told by this doctrine how much is too much, how much is too little, nor how to find out; in other words, Aristotle's notion is too abstract to be useful in solving practical questions of just compensation. We are left wondering what problems Aristotle thought he could help us solve by using his doctrine of the mean.

Aristotle's central notion of distributive justice is introduced early in Chapter 3 by his remark that "the just is equal, as all men suppose it to be, even apart from argument." However, as the subsequent discussion immediately shows, Aristotle is no *egalitarian;* he does not believe that justice requires men to be treated equally and that institutions are just only in so far as they achieve this outcome. He is quick to point out that justice must be guided by desert or merit, and therefore depart from strict equality. His theory of justice (like Plato's before him) is obviously *meritarian.* The idea that justice consists in rendering to each man what is due him was not new in Aristotle's day, and it has survived him (as seen in a passing allusion of Hobbes) in the maxim credited to the Roman jurist, Ulpian, *justitia est constans et perpetua voluntas ius suum cuique tribuendi* ("justice is the constant and perpetual will to render to each what is due him"). Since Aristotle believed that all men differ in their merits, and therefore in what they deserve, he is led to repudiate the egalitarian ideal of equal portions in favor of what he calls "geometrical proportion," or proportionate equality. What he has in mind can be seen by considering the egalitarian maxims, "Share and share alike," and "One man, one vote." For Aristotle, these maxims command what he would have called an "arithmetical proportion" between goods or votes, to distribute them in the ratio 1:1. Such a distribution would not, in his view, be a just one, except in the special case where the persons in question were equals. "Share and share alike" directs us to ignore all differences among persons as irrelevant to the allotment of portions. Aristotle insists that persons differ in what they deserve because of some decisive fact about their relative merit. From among various possibilities he mentions free and noble birth and wealth as likely to deserve special consideration. Proportionate equality, in effect, requires us to apportion shares of distributable goods justly according to the relative "weight" of the person involved, a large share for a "large" person and a small share for a "small" person. Yet it would be a mistake to see in Aristotle's doctrine of proportionate equality a denial of the spirit or the letter of his own remark that "the just is equal." He did not believe, as Hobbes and Mill did, that all men are "equal by nature;" and he did believe that justice can never discount the relative inferiorities and superiorities to be seen among men. Here, as we shall see later (in the final selection in this volume), Aristotle is more modern than at first he seems. His theory, of course, does not preclude treating all men justly by treating them all exactly equally. He makes no explicit provision for what he would regard as the remote possibility that all men *deserve* equal treatment because they are, in every relevant respect, equals. When he says elsewhere (*Politics,* III. 9) that justice requires equal treatment for equals, and unequal treatment for unequals, he reveals that he takes for granted the natural inequality of men and the inevitability of social inequalities as well, and that he is in no wise persuaded by these inequalities to conclude that all such inequalities are unjust or that justice is forever beyond our reach. Aristotle's theory escapes the contempt Orwell's *Animal Farm* taught us to visit on the swinish credo: "All are equal, but some are more equal than others." This is so because he does not pretend to an egalitarian bias; he is frankly aristocratic and anti-democratic. The two dozen centuries since his time have produced few theories of justice which disagree with his fundamental point that there are just inequalities. The dispute is confined to the question of which inequalities are the unjust ones and what criterion shows them to be unjust. This dispute is the unifying theme of all the selections in this volume, and it is fitting that Aristotle's meritarian theory of justice should set the topic for what follows.

When we turn to Hobbes' great treatise, *Leviathan,* we find a theory of justice and equality set within a comprehensive doctrine of "laws of nature," a variant of the Natural Law tradition common to thinkers as diverse as St. Thomas Aquinas and John Locke, and traceable to Aristotle's notion of "natural justice." Natural laws, Hobbes claims, are "immutable and eternal" and therefore apply to everyone everywhere. There is intended an analogy between these social laws and the laws of elementary mechanics. Hobbes would have argued that the Law of Falling Bodies is true of all physical objects, terrestrial and celestial, large and small. Likewise, there must be laws of man's "motions" or conduct which have no boundaries in race, climate, or region. But that is not all. Any true generalizations about human conduct qualify as laws of nature in Hobbes' sense only if they meet a further test, namely, that their universal adoption is necessary to the peace and security of all concerned, and their neglect or violation leads to social disharmony, strife, and, if the violations are widespread and continuous, ruin. Hobbes' nineteen laws of nature, therefore, can be viewed as empirical generalizations of the sort that, today, we might expect from sociological or anthropological research. They are open to possible criticism on the ground that one or more of them fails when tested by the evidence and therefore is not a "law" at all; also, there may be other laws which do meet the test of experience but are not mere corollaries of those on his list. We must also note that Hobbes' laws of nature are typically framed not in the language of empirical generalization but in words of general admonition, as though God Himself in all His sovereign majesty had spoken to men and laid down these rules for their mutual conduct (for their own good, of course) and ordered them to obey on pain of death. In one passage, Hobbes suggests that this is precisely how we should understand these laws as laws *for* us (*Leviathan,* I. 15, end). It is upon this general theory of the laws of nature, with their dual character as empirical generalizations and as sovereign commands, that Hobbes bases his theory of justice.

The contrasts between Hobbes and Aristotle on justice and equality are striking and of fundamental importance. Justice, according to Hobbes, is "keeping valid covenants" (third law), and equality is simply a "natural" fact about men (ninth law). Hobbes plainly declares elsewhere (in *Leviathan,* I. 13) that all men are gifted with roughly equivalent "faculties of body and mind," so that social advantages and disadvantages apart, there is no rational basis for any man to see himself as naturally inferior to any other man. (Why Hobbes thinks men are by nature equal and whether he is right are matters the reader may prefer to ponder after he has studied the essay by Bernard Williams.) This natural equality among men has inescapable moral significance, though Hobbes does not dwell on it. For one thing, it clearly provides a presumption in favor of equal treatment in the absence of some basis for special preferment of one person over another. It also provides an assumption for Hobbes' distinctive notion of justice. We owe to him, perhaps more than to any previous thinker, the view that justice is to be found primarily in doing whatever free, rational, and equal persons agree, or in his words, "covenant," to do. Naturally, therefore, Hobbes allots considerable energy to a careful explanation of what a covenant is. That persons may enter into such agreements for the most selfish of motives and that they will often attempt to cheat on their committments Hobbes not only does not deny, he insists upon it. It is for this reason (one of his deepest convictions about human nature) that men must accept "a common power"—a government—"with right and force sufficient to compel performance." As he adds later (in *Leviathan,* II. 17), "covenants without the sword are but words." Yet he knows that our selfishness and irrationality in no way affect the obligation to perform as promised when it comes time to do so. The distinctive morality of justice in Hobbes' theory lies in the sense of obligation of those who see that they are morally bound to do what they have freely agreed to do (though Hobbes does not insist on the adverb "freely"). It is this conception of justice which provides the germinal idea developed with such penetration and scope in the essay reprinted below by John Rawls.

Whereas Aristotle developed a theory of proportionate equality in order to accommodate his conviction that there are just inequalities, Hobbes' theory accomplishes the same result but in quite another way. His egalitarian committments end prior to the point where men contract agreements with one another (this is in no way mitigated by his emphasis upon impartiality in the eleventh law of nature). Whatever inequalities result from the activities of contracting parties are, in Hobbes' theory, fully justified. They are superimposed upon the natural equality of men by a series of just acts and so cannot possibly constitute unjust inequalities. Again, the tacit difference in social outlook between Aristotle's theory and Hobbes' is striking and unmistakable. It is the difference between a stable social order based on due respect for the well-nigh unalterable differences among men owing to their birth, family, and status, in contrast to the industry and ingenuity of a rising middle class engaged in forming partnerships, corporations, and other combinations in order to exploit nature (and one another) and to reap the profits. The outcome of men's "covenants," their reassessment when one of the parties sees he has been taken unfair advantage of, or when he realizes that he has bargained himself into a serious disadvantage, or when the consequences of private contractual enterprise prove socially disastrous—on these possibilities Hobbes wastes no concern at all. It may be possible to extract from his interest in peace and security a set of reasons for challenging unfair, unequal, and (we would say) unjust results of freely undertaken agreements. But Hobbes, in classic liberal fashion, does not do so: *pacta sunt servanda ruat coelum.*

No doubt one of the most disputed features of Hobbes' theory of justice is that, despite its heavy emphasis on laws natural and positive, it seems to provide us with absolutely no way of challenging any such law on grounds of injustice. At one point in *Leviathan,* Hobbes bluntly says, "no law can be unjust" (II. 30); if we study his theory of sovereignty we can understand his reasons for this position. But it follows from his general theory that the notion of an "unjust law," a term we constantly find on our lips and in our thoughts as we appraise the political and legal structures around us, simply makes no sense. It is all very well to define "justice" as Hobbes does, so that it has explicit application only to the keeping of contracts and covenants; but if it is a consequence of this that we cannot even sensibly try to criticize laws for their justice or injustice, we are likely to find such a definition (as have most of Hobbes' successors) unacceptable.

The difficulty is not that Hobbes provided no implicit criterion in terms of which to appraise the positive laws of a political community, for he did. Although he nowhere puts it quite so directly, we can see that, on his view, it is the usefulness to mankind of rules such as "Keep your word!" which explains our permanent interest in justice and the high seriousness which moralists and philosophers alike have always attached to performing our just obligations. For Hobbes, then, as for many other thinkers, to raise questions about the justice of any law or moral rule is always in the end to raise a question about the social utility of that law or rule. It remained for Hobbes' utilitarian successors to work out in closer detail precisely how and why utility is related both to justice and to equality.

John Stuart Mill's position, reprinted from his famous essay, *Utilitarianism,* is one of the classic statements of a utilitarian theory of justice and equality. Of special value to the reader who may be new to moral philosophy is Mill's list of different "modes of action," in which he thinks we can see five clear cases of justice and injustice. His examples will suggest others and thereby provide a body of data, as it were, against which to test both one's own intuitions on justice and the theories of Mill and others as well. Mill thinks his examples can be adequately understood only on his own theory. His central thesis he expresses near the end of the selection in these words: "Justice is a name for certain moral requirements, which, regarded collectively, stand higher in the scale of social utility, and are therefore of more paramount obligation, than any others. . . ."

Two main features of his argument should be noted. First, he insists (what is surely true) that the expedient or useful is not coextensive with the moral, and that the moral likewise encompasses far more than the just. Yet near the opening of his remarks, he says, "the dictates of justice coincide with a part of the field of general expediency." How, then, are the three (the expedient, the moral, the just) related? According to Mill, the difference between approving of some act as expedient and approving of it as morally required is that in the latter sort of case we would feel gratified at someone being "compelled" to do what he is required to do; whereas the difference between moral approval of an act and approving of it as just is that in the latter case a person's failure to do the act in question would involve violating "the rights" of another. Mere inexpediency or inutility in an act does not provoke us to wish compulsion (or punishment) upon the agent, much less lead us to condemn him for violating the rights of others. Second, Mill believes that justice, as understood by the ordinary man, "is not some one rule, principle, or maxim, but many," and that in case after case these rules conflict. The result is "confusion," from which he perhaps too readily concludes, "there is no other mode of extrication than the utilitarian." His illustrations, drawn from controversies surrounding just punishments, fair wages, and equitable taxation, are designed to show the sceptical that the Principle of Utility is a more fundamental moral principle than justice because it alone can arbitrate among the dictates of equally plausible but rival principles of justice. It would be irrational, Mill implies, to try to settle such disputes without any reference to the utility of the possible solutions, and it would be arbitrary to rely in such cases upon one rather than another of the several conflicting "rules, principles, or maxims" of justice. While it would be an exaggeration to say that Mill's chief thesis stands or falls on the success of these two arguments, they are an integral part of the way he chooses to develop his overall theory.

Mill has much else to offer on behalf of his attempted reduction of justice to utility (or, as Rawls says, to "efficiency"), notably, the acknowledgement that there is nothing moral whatsoever in our "sentiment of justice," because it is the naked desire for "retaliation" and "vengeance" against those who have inflicted injustices upon us. But Mill's somewhat obscure theory does not begin to compare in subtlety with the chief ideas Hume had brought to his own (by no means dogmatic) utilitarian theory of justice a century before. The brief excerpts reprinted here from Hume's *Treatise* and his second *Enquiry* do not adequately convey his entire theory, but they do show several valuable qualifications and alternatives to Mill's position (and for this reason Hume has been placed out of chronological sequence and appears after the selection from Mill). By emphasizing the environmental conditions under which justice could become "totally useless" and by distinguishing sharply between the utility of a "single act" and the utility of "the whole scheme or system" of which the act is but one instance, Hume measurably sophisticates any utilitarian theory of justice. Hume also has the better of Mill on the question of how a utilitarian can incorporate a principle of equality. Mill tells us early in his remarks that "each person maintains that equality is the dictate of justice, except where he thinks that expediency requires inequality." This is sufficient to place Mill within the egalitarian tradition, even though it shows that equality is not one of his first principles. Yet Mill goes on to say that the general utility of impartiality and equality is shown by the fact that these ideas are "involved in the very meaning of utility, or the greatest happiness principle." This is singularly implausible for Mill to assert, given his theory of just inequalities. Hume offers a much better argument in this passage in his *Enquiry* in which he notices what today would be called the diminishing marginal utility of inequality: "frivolous vanity in one individual frequently costs more than bread to many families." (It is this view, interestingly enough, which is more familiar to us today in the words, "None should have luxuries while any lack necessities," a maxim of socialist justice that would have aroused Hume's abhorrence.) This and other points where Hume improves upon Mill and Hobbes have been subtly reworked in the theory of justice developed by John Rawls.

Rawls' essay, as I have already indicated, is the pivotal one in the volume because in it the central issues of the nature of justice, equality, their relationship to each other, and their foundation in human nature, are developed out of reflections to be found in such different philosophers as Aristotle and Hobbes (whom Rawls does not mention) and Hume and Mill (whom he does). This essay is also by far the most widely discussed of any contemporary philosophical investigation of justice and equality. The reader will find an especially vivid illustration of Rawls' differences with the classic utilitarians in the seventh section of his essay in which he claims to prove that "slavery is *always* unjust." A utilitarian cannot reach such a final condemnation of this (or, for that matter, any other) social practice. This is but one application of the two "principles" of justice which Rawls presents in the second section of his essay and which in turn depend on the "theorem" he seeks to prove at the end of the third section.

Early in his essay, Rawls remarks that we must distinguish between "that sense of equality which is an aspect of the concept of justice from that sense of equality which belongs to a more comprehensive social ideal." He indicates that his essay is confined to equality in the former sense, as is true of all the writers in the selections which precede his. The final four selections redress the balance by probing for the sources and difficulties in egalitarianism as "a comprehensive social ideal." The essays by Williams, Lucas, and Benn, as I mentioned at the beginning, are sufficiently straightforward in what they undertake and intimately related to each other that introductory comments on them here is quite unnecessary. If the reader wishes he may turn at this point to the final essay in the volume in which I attempt to set out the chief ideas which make up egalitarianism. There the broad outlines of the issues to which Williams, Lucas, and Benn address themselves are discussed by way of a critique of "radical" egalitarianism.

ARISTOTLE

Justice

1

With regard to justice and injustice we must consider (1) what kind of actions they are concerned with, (2) what sort of mean justice is, and (3) between what extremes the just act is intermediate. Our investigation shall follow the same course as the preceding discussions.

We see that all men mean by justice that kind of state of character which makes people disposed to do what is just and makes them act justly and wish for what is just; and similarly by injustice that state which makes them act unjustly and wish for what is unjust. Let us too, then, lay this down as a general basis. For the same is not true of the sciences and the faculties as of states of character. A faculty or a science which is one and the same is held to relate to contrary objects, but a state of character which is one of two contraries does *not* produce the contrary results; for example as a result of health we do not do what is the opposite of healthy, but only what is healthy; for we say a man walks healthily, when he walks as a healthy man would.

Now often one contrary state is recognized from its contrary, and often states are recognized from the subjects that exhibit them;

The Oxford Translation of Aristotle, ed. W. D. Ross, Volume IX, *The Nichomachean Ethics* (tr. W. D. Ross, 1925), Book V, Chapters 1–7, 10. Reprinted by permission. Some of the translator's notes have been omitted and others have been added from the *World's Classics* edition published by Oxford University Press in 1954.

for (a) if good condition is known, bad condition also becomes known, and (b) good condition is known from the things that are in good condition, and they from it. If good condition is firmness of flesh, it is necessary both that bad condition should be flabbiness of flesh and that the wholesome should be that which causes firmness in flesh. And it follows for the most part that if one contrary is ambiguous the other also will be ambiguous; for example if "just" is so, that "unjust" will be so too.

Now "justice" and "injustice" seem to be ambiguous, but because their different meanings approach near to one another the ambiguity escapes notice and is not obvious as it is, comparatively, when the meanings are far apart, for example (for here the difference in outward form is great) as the ambiguity in the use of *kleis* for the collar-bone of an animal and for that with which we lock a door. Let us take as a starting-point, then, the various meanings of "an unjust man." Both the lawless man and the grasping and unfair man are thought to be unjust, so that evidently both the law-abiding and the fair man will be just. The just, then, is the lawful and the fair, the unjust the unlawful and the unfair.

Since the unjust man is grasping, he must be concerned with goods—not all goods, but those with which prosperity and adversity have to do, which taken absolutely are always good, but for a particular person are not always good. Now men pray for and pursue these things; but they should not, but should pray that the things that are good absolutely may also be good for them, and should choose the things that *are* good for them. The unjust man does not always choose the greater, but also the less—in the case of things bad absolutely; but because the lesser evil is itself thought to be in a sense good, and graspingness is directed at the good, therefore he is thought to be grasping. And he is unfair; for this contains and is common to both.

Since the lawless man was seen to be unjust and the law-abiding man just, evidently all lawful acts are in a sense just acts; for the acts laid down by the legislative art are lawful, and each of these, we say, is just. Now the laws in their enactments on all subjects aim at the common advantage either of all or of the best or of those who hold power, or something of the sort; so that in one sense we call those acts just that tend to produce and preserve happiness and its components for the political society. And the law bids us do both the acts of a brave man (*e.g.* not to desert our post nor take to flight nor throw away our arms), and those of a temperate man (*e.g.* not to commit adultery nor to gratify one's lust), and those of a good-tempered man (*e.g.* not to strike another nor to speak evil), and similarly with regard to the other virtues and forms of wickedness, commanding some acts and forbidding others; and the rightly-framed law does this rightly, and the hastily conceived one less well.

This form of justice, then, is complete virtue, but not absolutely, but in relation to our neighbour. And therefore justice is often thought to be the greatest of virtues, and "neither evening nor morning star" is so wonderful; and proverbially "in justice is every virtue comprehended." And it is complete virtue in its fullest sense, because it is the actual exercise of complete virtue. It is complete because he who possesses it can exercise his virtue not only in himself but towards his neighbour also; for many men can exercise virtue in their own affairs, but not in their relations to their neighbour. This is why the saying of Bias is thought to be true, that "rule will show the man;" for a ruler is necessarily in relation to other men and a member of a society. For this same reason justice, alone of the virtues, is thought to be "another's good," because it is related to our neighbour; for it does what is advantageous to another, either a ruler or a copartner. Now the worst man is he who exercises his wickedness both towards himself and towards his friends, and the best man is not he who exercises his virtue towards himself but he who exercises it towards another; for this is a difficult task. Justice in this sense, then, is not part of virtue but virtue entire, nor is the contrary injustice a part of vice but vice entire. What the difference is between virtue and justice in this sense is plain from what we have said; they are the same but their essence is not the same; what, as a relation to one's neighbour, is justice is, as a certain kind of state without qualification, virtue.

2

But at all events what we are investigating is the justice which is a *part* of virtue; for there is a justice of this kind, as we maintain. Similarly it is with injustice in the particular sense that we are concerned.

That there is such a thing is indicated by the fact that while the man who exhibits in action the other forms of wickedness acts wrongly indeed, but not graspingly (*e.g.* the man who throws away his shield through cowardice or speaks harshly through bad temper or fails to help a friend with money through meanness), when a man acts graspingly he often exhibits none of these vices—no, nor all together, but certainly wickedness of some kind (for we blame him) and injustice. There is, then, another kind of injustice which is a part of injustice in the wide sense, and a use of the word "unjust" which answers to a part of what is unjust in the wide sense of "contrary to the law." Again, if one man commits adultery for the sake of gain and makes money by it, while another does so at the bidding of appetite though he loses money and is penalized for it, the latter would be held to be self-indulgent rather than grasping, but the former is unjust, but not self-indulgent; evidently, therefore, he is unjust by reason of his making gain by his act. Again, all other unjust acts are ascribed invariably to some particular kind of wickedness, for example adultery to self-indulgence, the desertion of a comrade in battle to cowardice, physical violence to anger; but if a man makes gain, his action is ascribed to no form of wickedness but injustice. Evidently, therefore, there is apart from injustice in the wide sense another, "particular," injustice which shares the name and nature of the first, because its definition falls within the same genus; for the significance of both consists in a relation to one's neighbour, but the one is concerned with honour or money or safety—or that which includes all these, if we had a single name for it—and its motive is the pleasure that arises from gain; while the other is concerned with all the objects with which the good man is concerned.

It is clear, then, that there is more than one kind of justice, and that there is one which is distinct from virtue entire; we must try to grasp its genus and differentia.

The unjust has been divided into the unlawful and the unfair, and the just into the lawful and the fair. To the unlawful answers the afore-mentioned sense of injustice. But since the unfair and the unlawful are not the same, but are different as a part is from its whole (for all that is unfair is unlawful, but not all that is unlawful is unfair), the unjust and injustice in the sense of the unfair are not the same as but different from the former kind, as part from whole; for injustice in this sense is a part of injustice in the wide sense, and similarly justice in the one sense of justice in the other. Therefore we must speak also about particular justice and particular injustice, and similarly about the just and the unjust. The justice, then, which answers to the whole of virtue, and the corresponding injustice, one being the exercise of virtue as a whole, and the other that of vice as a whole, towards one's neighbour, we may leave on one side. And how the meanings of "just" and "unjust" which answer to these are to be distinguished is evident; for practically the majority of the acts commanded by the law are those which are prescribed from the point of view of virtue taken as a whole; for the law bids us practise every virtue and forbids us to practise any vice. And the things that tend to produce virtue taken as a whole are those of the acts prescribed by the law which have been prescribed with a view to education for the common good. But with regard to the education of the individual as such, which makes him without qualification a good *man*, we must determine later whether this is the function of the political art or of another; for perhaps it is not the same to be a good man and a good citizen of any state taken at random.

Of particular justice and that which is just in the corresponding sense, (A) one kind is that which is manifested in distributions of honour or money or the other things that fall to be divided among those who have a share in the constitution (for in these it is possible for one man to have a share either unequal or equal to that of another), and (B) one is that which plays a rectifying part in transactions between man and man. Of this there are two divisions; of transactions (1) some are voluntary and (2) others involuntary —voluntary such transactions as sale, purchase, loan for consumption, pledging, loan for use, depositing, letting (they are called voluntary because the origin of these transactions is voluntary), while of the involuntary (a) some are clandestine, such as theft, adultery, poisoning, procuring, enticement of slaves, assassination, false witness, and (b) others are violent, such as assault, imprisonment, murder, robbery with violence, mutilation, abuse, insult.

3

(A) We have shown that both the unjust man and the unjust act are unfair or unequal; now it is clear that there is also an intermediate between the two unequals involved in either case. And this is the equal; for in any kind of action in which there is a more and a less there is also what is equal. If, then, the unjust is unequal, the just is equal, as all men suppose it to be, even apart from argument. And since the equal is intermediate, the just will be an intermediate. Now equality implies at least two things. The just, then, must be both intermediate and equal and relative (*i.e.* for certain persons). And *qua* intermediate it must be between certain things (which are respectively greater and less); *qua* equal, it involves *two* things; *qua* just, it is for certain people. The just, therefore, involves at least four terms; for the persons for whom it is in fact just are two, and the things in which it is manifested, the objects distributed, are two. And the same equality will exist between the persons and between the things concerned; for as the latter—the things concerned—are related, so are the former; if they are not equal, they will not have what is equal, but this is the origin of quarrels and complaints—when either equals have and are awarded unequal shares, or unequals equal shares. Further, this is plain from the fact that awards should be "according to merit;" for all men agree that what is just in distribution must be according to merit in some sense, though they do not all specify the same sort of merit, but democrats identify it with the status of freeman, supporters of oligarchy with wealth (or with noble birth), and supporters of aristocracy with excellence.

The just, then, is a species of the proportionate (proportion being not a property only of the kind of number which consists of abstract units, but of number in general). For proportion is equality of ratios, and involves four terms at least (that discrete proportion involves four terms is plain, but so does continuous proportion, for it uses one term as two and mentions it twice; for example "as the line A is to the line B, so is the line B to the line C;" the line B, then, has been mentioned twice, so that if the line B be assumed twice, the proportional terms will be four); and the just, too, involves at least four terms, and the ratio between one pair is the same as that between the other pair; for there is a similar distinction between the persons and between the things. As the term A, then, is to B, so will C be to D, and therefore, *alternando,* as A is to C, B will be to D. Therefore also the whole is in the same ratio to the whole;[1] and this coupling the distribution effects and, if the terms are so combined, effects justly. The conjunction, then,

[1] Person A + thing C to person B + thing D.

of the term A with C and of B with D is what is just in distribution,[2] and this species of the just is intermediate, and the unjust is what violates the proportion; for the proportional is intermediate, and the just is proportional. (Mathematicians call this kind of proportion geometrical; for it is in geometrical proportion that it follows that the whole is to the whole as either part is to the corresponding part.) This proportion is not continuous; for we cannot get a single term standing for a person and a thing.

This, then, is what the just is—the proportional; the unjust is what violates the proportion. Hence one term becomes too great, the other too small, as indeed happens in practice; for the man who acts unjustly has too much, and the man who is unjustly treated too little, of what is good. In the case of evil the reverse is true; for the lesser evil is reckoned a good in comparison with the greater evil, since the lesser evil is rather to be chosen than the greater, and what is worthy of choice is good, and what is worthier of choice a greater good.

This, then, is one species of the just.

4

(B) The remaining one is the rectificatory, which arises in connexion with transactions both voluntary and involuntary. This form of the just has a different specific character from the former. For the justice which distributes common possessions is always in accordance with the kind of proportion mentioned above (for in the case also in which the distribution is made from the common funds of a partnership it will be according to the same ratio which the funds put into the business by the partners bear to one another); and the injustice opposed to this kind of justice is that which violates the proportion. But the justice in transactions between man and man is a sort of equality indeed, and the injustice a sort of inequality; not according to that kind of proportion,

[2] The problem of distributive justice is to divide the distributable honour or reward into parts which are to one another as are the merits of the persons who are to participate. If
A (first person) : B (second person) :: C (first portion) : D (second portion),
then (*alternando*) A : C :: B : D,
and therefore (*componendo*) A + C : B + D :: A : B.
In other words the position established answers to the relative merits of the parties.

however, but according to arithmetical proportion.[3] For it makes no difference whether a good man has defrauded a bad man or a bad man a good one, nor whether it is a good or a bad man that has committed adultery; the law looks only to the distinctive character of the injury, and treats the parties as equal, if one is in the wrong and the other is being wronged, and if one inflicted injury and the other has received it. Therefore, this kind of injustice being an inequality, the judge tries to equalize it; for in the case also in which one has received and the other has inflicted a wound, or one has slain and the other been slain, the suffering and the action have been unequally distributed; but the judge tries to equalize things by means of the penalty, taking away from the gain of the assailant. For the term "gain" is applied generally to such cases, even if it be not a term appropriate to certain cases, for example to the person who inflicts a wound—and "loss" to the sufferer; at all events when the suffering has been estimated, the one is called loss and the other gain. Therefore the equal is intermediate between the greater and the less, but the gain and the loss are respectively greater and less in contrary ways; more of the good and less of the evil are gain, and the contrary is loss; intermediate between them is, as we saw, the equal, which we say is just; therefore corrective justice will be the intermediate between loss and gain. This is why, when people dispute, they take refuge in the judge; and to go to the judge is to go to justice; for the nature of the judge is to be a sort of animate justice; and they seek the judge as an intermediate, and in some states they call judges mediators, on the assumption that if they get what is intermediate they will get what is just. The just, then, is an intermediate, since the judge is so. Now the judge restores equality; it is as though there were a line divided into unequal parts, and he took away that by which

[3] The problem of "rectificatory justice" has nothing to do with punishment proper but is only that of rectifying a wrong that has been done, by awarding damages; *i.e.* rectificatory justice is that of the civil, not that of the criminal courts. The parties are treated by the court as equal (since a law court is not a court of morals), and the wrongful act is reckoned as having brought equal gain to the wrong-doer and loss to his victim; it brings A to the position $A + C$, and B to the position $B - C$. The judge's task is to find the arithmetical mean between these, and this he does by transferring C from A to B. Thus (A being treated as $= B$) we get the arithmetical "proportion"

$$(A + C) - (A + C - C) = (A + C - C) - (B - C)$$

or

$$(A + C) - (B - C + C) = (B - C + C) - (B - C).$$

the greater segment exceeds the half, and added it to the smaller segment. And when the whole has been equally divided, then they say they have "their own" that is, when they have got what is equal. The equal is intermediate between the greater and the lesser line according to arithmetical proportion. It is for this reason also that it is called just (*dikaion*), because it is a division into two equal parts (*dicha*), just as if one were to call it (*dichaion*); and the judge (*dicastes*) is one who bisects (*dichastes*). For when something is subtracted from one of two equals and added to the other, the other is in excess by these two; since if what was taken from the one had not been added to the other, the latter would have been in excess by one only. It therefore exceeds the intermediate by one, and the intermediate exceeds by one that from which something was taken. By this, then, we shall recognize both what we must subtract from that which has more, and what we must add to that which has less; we must add to the latter that by which the intermediate exceeds it, and subtract from the greatest that by which it exceeds the intermediate. Let the lines AA′, BB′, CC′ be equal to one another; from the line AA′ let the segment AE have been subtracted, and to the line CC′ let the segment CD [*sc,* equal to AE] have been added, so that the whole line DCC′ exceeds the line EA′ by the segment CD and the segment CF; therefore it exceeds the line BB′ by the segment CD.

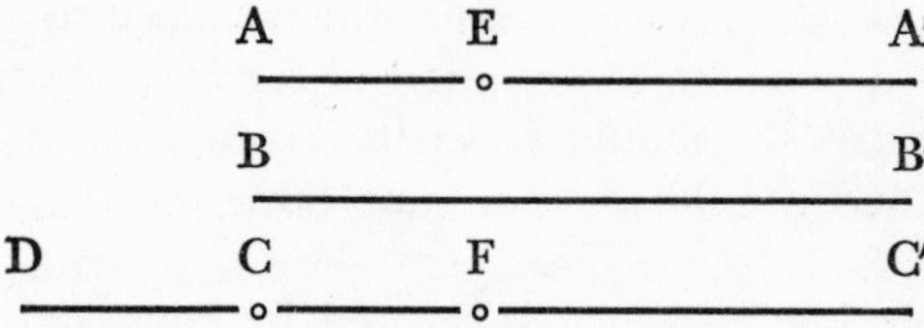

A E A′

B B′

D C F C′

These names, both loss and gain, have come from voluntary exchange; for to have more than one's own is called gaining, and to have less than one's original share is called losing, for example in buying and selling and in all other matters in which the law has left people free to make their own terms; but when they get neither more nor less but just what belongs to themselves, they say that they have their own and that they neither lose nor gain.

Therefore the just is intermediate between a sort of gain and a sort of loss, namely those which are involuntary [*i.e.* for the loser];

it consists in having an equal amount before and after the transaction.

5

Some think that *reciprocity* is without qualification just, as the Pythagoreans said; for they defined justice without qualification as reciprocity. Now "reciprocity" fits neither distributive nor rectificatory justice—yet people *want* even the justice of Rhadamanthus to mean this:

Should a man suffer what he did, right justice would be done

—for in many cases reciprocity and rectificatory justice are not in accord, for example (1) if an official has inflicted a wound, he should not be wounded in return, and if some one has wounded an official, he ought not to be wounded only but punished in addition. Further (2) there is a great difference between a voluntary and an involuntary act. But in associations for exchange this sort of justice does hold men together—reciprocity in accordance with a proportion and not on the basis of precisely equal return. For it is by proportionate requital that the city holds together. Men seek to return either evil for evil—and if they cannot do so, think their position mere slavery—or good for good—and if they cannot do so there is no exchange, but it is by exchange that they hold together. This is why they give a prominent place to the temple of the Graces—to promote the requital of services; for this is characteristic of grace—we should serve in return one who has shown grace to us, and should another time take the initiative in showing it.

Now proportionate return is secured by cross-conjunction.[4] Let A be a builder, B a shoemaker, C a house, D a shoe. The builder, then, must get from the shoemaker the latter's work, and must himself give him in return his own. If, then, first there is propor-

[4] The working of proportionate reciprocity is not very clearly described by Aristotle, but seems to be as follows. A and B are workers in different trades, and will normally be of different degrees of worth. Their products, therefore, will also have unequal worth, *i.e.* (though Aristotle does not expressly reduce the question to one of time) if $A = nB$ (what A makes, say, in an hour) will be worth n times as much as D (what B makes in an hour). A fair exchange will then take place if A gets nD and B gets 1 C; *i.e.,* if A gives what it takes him an hour to make, in exchange for what it takes B n hours to make.

tionate equality of goods, and then reciprocal action takes place, the result we mention will be effected. If not, the bargain is not equal, and does not hold; for there is nothing to prevent the work of the one being better than that of the other; they must therefore be equated. (And this is true of the other arts also; for they would have been destroyed if what the patient suffered had not been just what the agent did, and of the same amount and kind.[5]) For it is not two doctors that associate for exchange, but a doctor and a farmer, or in general people who are different and unequal; but these must be equated. This is why all things that are exchanged must be somehow comparable. It is for this end that money has been introduced, and it becomes in a sense an intermediate; for it measures all things, and therefore the excess and the defect—how many shoes are equal to a house or to a given amount of food. The number of shoes exchanged for a house [or for a given amount of food] must therefore correspond to the ratio of builder to shoemaker. For if this be not so, there will be no exchange and no intercourse. And this proportion will not be effected unless the goods are somehow equal. All goods must therefore be measured by some one thing, as we said before.[6] Now this unit is in truth demand, which holds all things together (for if men did not need one another's goods at all, or did not need them equally, there would be either no exchange or not the same exchange); but money has become by convention a sort of representative of demand; and this is why it has the name "money" (*nomisma*)—because it exists not by nature but by law (*nomos*) and it is in our power to change

[5] This sentence conveys a natural enough thought, and echoes closely the language of Plato, *Gorgias,* 476 B–D. But it seems to have no relevance to the context, and probably we have here the unsuccessful attempt of an early editor to find a suitable place for an isolated note of Aristotle's.

[6] Aristotle's meaning, which has caused much difficulty, seems to be explained by a reference to *Nichomachean Ethics,* Book IX, chap. 1. That chapter concludes with the observation that ". . . the receiver should assess a thing not at what it seems worth when he has it, but at what he assessed it at before he had it." The reasoning in that chapter shows that Aristotle's meaning here must be that people must not exchange goods in random amounts and *then* bring themselves into a "figure of proportion." For each will then set an unduly high value on the goods he has parted with and an unduly low value on those he has received; and any adjustment that is made will be decided by their respective powers of bluff. One party will have "both excesses over the other, since what he gets will exceed the mean and what the other man gets will fall short of it (*cf.* the end of chap. 4, *supra*). The only fair method is for each to set a value on his own and on the other's goods *before* they exchange, and for them to come to an agreement if they can.

it and make it useless. There will, then, be reciprocity when the terms have been equated so that as farmer is to shoemaker, the amount of the shoemaker's work is to that of the farmer's work for which it exchanges. But we must not bring them into a figure of proportion when they have already exchanged (otherwise one extreme will have both excesses), but when they still have their own goods. Thus they are equals and associates just because this equality can be effected in their case. Let A be a farmer, C food, B a shoemaker, D his product equated to C. If it had not been possible for reciprocity to be thus effected, there would have been no association of the parties. That demand holds things together as a single unit is shown by the fact that when men do not need one another, that is when neither needs the other or one does not need the other, they do not exchange, as we do when some one wants what one has oneself, for example when people permit the exportation of corn in exchange for wine. This equation therefore must be established. And for the future exchange—that if we do not need a thing now we shall have it if ever we do need it—money is as it were our surety; for it must be possible for us to get what we want by bringing the money. Now the same thing happens to money itself as to goods—it is not always worth the same; yet it tends to be steadier. This is why all goods must have a price set on them; for then there will always be exchange, and if so, association of man with man. Money, then, acting as a measure, makes goods commensurate and equates them; for neither would there have been association if there were not exchange, nor exchange if there were not equality, nor equality if there were not commensurability. Now in truth it is impossible that things differing so much should become commensurate, but with reference to demand they may become so sufficiently. There must, then, be a unit, and that fixed by agreement (for which reason it is called money); for it is this that makes all things commensurate, since all things are measured by money. Let A be a house, B ten minae, C a bed. A is half of B, if the house is worth five minae or equal to them; the bed, C, is a tenth of B; it is plain, then, how many beds are equal to a house, namely five. That exchange took place thus before there was money is plain; for it makes no difference whether it is five beds that exchange for a house, or the money value of five beds.

We have now defined the unjust and the just. These having been marked off from each other, it is plain that just action is intermediate between acting unjustly and being unjustly treated; for the one is to have too much and the other to have too little. Justice is a kind of mean, but not in the same way as the other virtues, but because it relates to an intermedate amount, while injustice relates to the extremes. And justice is that in virtue of which the just man is said to be a doer, by choice, of that which is just, and one who will distribute either between himself and another or between two others not so as to give more of what is desirable to himself and less to his neighbour (and conversely with what is harmful), but so as to give what is equal in accordance with proportion; and similarly in distributing between two other persons. Injustice on the other hand is similarly related to the unjust, which is excess and defect, contrary to proportion, of the useful or hurtful. For which reason injustice is excess and defect, namely because it is productive of excess and defect—in one's own case excess of what is in its own nature useful and defect of what is hurtful, while in the case of others it is as a whole like what it is in one's own case, but proportion may be violated in either direction. In the unjust act to have too little is to be unjustly treated; to have too much is to act unjustly.

Let this be taken as our account of the nature of justice and injustice, and similarly of the just and the unjust in general.

6

Since acting unjustly does not necessarily imply being unjust, we must ask what sort of unjust acts imply that the doer is unjust with respect to each type of injustice, for example a thief, an adulterer, or a brigand. Surely the answer does not turn on the difference between these types. For a man might even lie with a woman knowing who she was, but the origin of his act might be not deliberate choice but passion. He acts unjustly, then, but is not unjust; for example a man is not a thief, yet he stole, nor an adulterer, yet he committed adultery; and similarly in all other cases.

Now we have previously stated how the reciprocal is related to the just; but we must not forget that what we are looking for is not only what is just without qualification but also political justice. This is found among men who share their life with a view to self-sufficiency, men who are free and either proportionately or arithmetically equal, so that between those who do not fulfil this condition there is no political justice but justice in a special sense and by analogy. For justice exists only between men whose mutual relations are governed by law; and law exists for men between whom there is injustice; for legal justice is the discrimination of the just and the unjust. And between men between whom there is injustice there is also unjust action (though there is not injustice between all between whom there is unjust action), and this is assigning too much to oneself of things good in themselves and too little of things evil in themselves. This is why we do not allow a *man* to rule, but *rational principle,* because a man behaves thus in his own interests and becomes a tyrant. The magistrate on the other hand is the guardian of justice, and, if of justice, then of equality also. And since he is assumed to have no more than his share, if he is just (for he does not assign to himself more of what is good in itself, unless such a share is proportional to his merits—so that it is for others that he labours, and it is for this reason that men, as we stated previously, say that justice is "another's good"), therefore a reward must be given him, and this is honour and privilege; but those for whom such things are not enough become tyrants.

The justice of a master and that of a father are not the same as the justice of citizens, though they are like it; for there can be no injustice in the unqualified sense towards things that are one's own, but a man's chattel, and his child until it reaches a certain age and sets up for itself, are as it were part of himself, and no one chooses to hurt himself (for which reason there can be no injustice towards oneself). Therefore the justice or injustice of citizens is not manifested in these relations; for it was as we saw according to law, and between people naturally subject to law, and these as we saw are people who have an equal share in ruling and being ruled. Hence justice can more truly be manifested towards a wife than towards children and chattels, for the former is household justice; but even this is different from political justice.

7

Of political justice part is natural, part legal—natural, that which everywhere has the same force and does not exist by people's thinking this or that; legal, that which is originally indifferent, but when it has been laid down is not indifferent, for example, that a prisoner's ransom shall be a mina, or that a goat and not two sheep shall be sacrificed, and again all the laws that are passed for particular cases, for example, sacrifice shall be made in honour of Brasidas, and the provisions of decrees. Now some think that all justice is of this sort, because that which is by nature is unchangeable and has everywhere the same force (as fire burns both here and in Persia), while they see change in the things recognized as just. This, however, is not true in this unqualified way, but is true in a sense; or rather, with the gods it is perhaps not true at all, while with us there is something that is just even by nature, yet all of it is changeable; but still some is by nature, some not by nature. It is evident which sort of thing, among things capable of being otherwise, is by nature; and which is not but is legal and conventional, assuming that both are equally changeable. And in all other things the same distinction will apply; by nature the right hand is stronger, yet it is possible that all men should come to be ambidextrous. The things which are just by virtue of convention and expediency are like measures; for wine and corn measures are not everywhere equal, but larger in wholesale and smaller in retail markets. Similarly, the things which are just not by nature but by human enactment are not everywhere the same, since constitutions also are not the same, though there is but one which is everywhere by nature the best.

Of things just and lawful each is related as the universal to its particulars; for the things that are done are many, but of *them* each is one, since it is universal.

There is a difference between the act of injustice and what is unjust, and between the act of justice and what is just; for a thing is unjust by nature or by enactment; and this very thing, when it has been done, is an act of injustice, but before it is done is not yet that but is unjust. So, too, with an act of justice (though the general term is rather "just action," and "act of justice" is applied to the correction of the act of injustice).

Each of these must later[7] be examined separately with regard to the nature and number of its species and the nature of the things with which it is concerned.

• • • • • • • • • • • •

[7] Possibly a reference to an intended (or now lost) book of the *Politics* on laws.

10

Our next subject is equity and the equitable (*to epieikes*), and their respective relations to justice and the just. For on examination they appear to be neither absolutely the same nor generically different; and while we sometimes praise what is equitable and the equitable man (so that we apply the name by way of praise even to instances of the other virtues, instead of "good," meaning by *epieikesteron* that a thing is better), at other times, when we reason it out, it seems strange if the equitable, being something different from the just, is yet praiseworthy; for either the just or the equitable is not good, if they are different; or, if both are good, they are the same.

These, then, are pretty much the considerations that give rise to the problem about the equitable; they are all in a sense correct and not opposed to one another; for the equitable, though it is better than one kind of justice, yet is just, and it is not as being a different class of thing that it is better than the just. The same thing, then, is just and equitable, and while both are good the equitable is superior. What creates the problem is that the equitable is just, but not the legally just but a correction of legal justice. The reason is that all law is universal but about some things it is not possible to make a universal statement which shall be correct. In those cases, then, in which it is necessary to speak universally, but not possible to do so correctly, the law takes the usual case, though it is not ignorant of the possibility of error. And it is none the less correct; for the error is not in the law nor in the legislator but in the nature of the thing, since the matter of practical affairs is of this kind from the start. When the law speaks universally, then, and a case arises on it which is not covered by the universal statement, then it is right, where the legislator fails us and has erred by over-simplicity, to correct the omission—to say what the legislator himself would have said had he been present, and would have put into his law if he had known. Hence the equitable is just, and better than one kind of justice—not better than absolute justice but better than the error that arises from the absoluteness of the statement. And this is the nature of the equitable, a correction of law where it is defective owing to its universality. In fact this is the reason why all things are not determined by law, namely that about some things it is impossible to lay down a law, so that a decree is needed. For when the thing is indefinite the rule also is indefinite, like the leaden rule used in making the Lesbian moulding; the rule adapts itself to the shape of the stone and is not rigid, and so too the decree is adapted to the facts.

It is plain, then, what the equitable is, and that it is just and is better than one kind of justice. It is evident also from this who the equitable man is; the man who chooses and does such acts, and is no stickler for his rights in a bad sense but tends to take less than his share though he has the law on his side, is equitable, and this state of character is equity, which is a sort of justice and not a different state of character.

THOMAS HOBBES

Justice and the Laws of Nature

. . . A LAW OF NATURE, *lex naturalis,* is a precept or general rule, found out by reason, by which a man is forbidden to do that which is destructive of his life or takes away the means of preserving the same and to omit that by which he thinks it may be best preserved. For though they that speak of this subject use to confound *jus* and *lex, right* and *law,* yet they ought to be distinguished; because RIGHT consists in liberty to do or to forbear, whereas LAW determines and binds to one of them; so that law and right differ as much as obligation and liberty, which in one and the same matter are inconsistent. And because the condition of man, . . . is a condition of war of every one against every one—in which case everyone is governed by his own reason and there is nothing he can make use of that may not be a help unto him in preserving his life against his enemies—it follows that in such a condition every man has a right to everything, even to one another's body. And therefore, as long as this natural right of every man to everything endures, there can be no security to any man, how strong or wise soever he be, of living out the time which nature ordinarily allows men to live. And consequently it is a precept or general rule of reason *that every man ought to endeavor peace, as far as he has hope of obtaining it; and when he cannot obtain it, that he may seek and*

From *Leviathan* (1651), Part I, chs. 14–15 (with omissions). Spelling and punctuation have been modernized, the paragraphing revised, the marginal notes of the original omitted. Italics and capitalization are as in the original. The "laws of nature" have been numbered consecutively with roman numerals for ease of reference.

use all helps and advantages of war. The first branch of which rule contains the first and fundamental law of nature, which is [I] *to seek peace and follow it.* The second, the sum of the right of nature, which is, *by all means we can to defend ourselves.*

From this fundamental law of nature, by which men are commanded to endeavor peace, is derived this second law: [II] *that a man be willing, when others are so too, as far forth as for peace and defense of himself he shall think it necessary, to lay down this right to all things, and be contented with so much liberty against other men as he would allow other men against himself.* For as long as every man holds this right of doing anything he likes, so long are all men in the condition of war. But if other men will not lay down their right as well as he, then there is no reason for anyone to divest himself of his, for that were to expose himself to prey, which no man is bound to, rather than to dispose himself to peace. This is that law of the gospel: *whatsoever you require that others should do to you, that do ye to them.* And that law of all men, *quod tibi fieri non vis, alteri ne feceris.*

To *lay down* a man's *right* to anything is to *divest* himself of the *liberty* of hindering another of the benefit of his own right to the same. For he that renounces or passes away his right gives not to any other man a right which he had not before—because there is nothing to which every man had not right by nature—but only stands out of his way, that he may enjoy his own original right without hindrance from him, not without hindrance from another. So that the effect which redounds to one man by another man's defect of right is but so much diminution of impediments to the use of his own right original. Right is laid aside either by simply renouncing it or by transferring it to another. By *simply* RENOUNCING, when he cares not to whom the benefit thereof redounds. By TRANSFERRING, when he intends the benefit thereof to some certain person or persons. And when a man has in either manner abandoned or granted away his right, then he is said to be OBLIGED or BOUND not to hinder those to whom such right is granted or abandoned from the benefit of it; and that he *ought,* and it is his DUTY, not to make void that voluntary act of his own; and that such hindrance is INJUSTICE and INJURY as being *sine jure,* the right being before renounced or transferred. So that *injury* or *injustice* in the controversies of the world is somewhat like to that which in the disputations of scholars is called *absurdity.* For as it is there called an absurdity to contradict what one maintained in the beginning, so in the world it is called injustice and injury voluntarily to undo that which from the beginning he had voluntarily done. The way by which a man either simply renounces or transfers his right is a declaration or signification by some voluntary and sufficient sign or signs that he does so renounce or transfer, or has so renounced or transferred, the same to him that accepts it. And these signs are either words only or actions only; or as it happens most often, both words and actions. And the same are the BONDS by which men are bound and obliged—bonds that have their strength, not from their own nature, for nothing is more easily broken than a man's word, but from fear of some evil consequence upon the rupture.

Whensoever a man transfers his right or renounces it, it is either in consideration of some right reciprocally transferred to himself or for some other good he hopes for thereby. For it is a voluntary act; and of the voluntary acts of every man, the object is some *good to himself*. And therefore there be some rights which no man can be understood by any words or other signs to have abandoned or transferred. As, first, a man cannot lay down the right of resisting them that assault him by force to take away his life, because he cannot be understood to aim thereby at any good to himself. The same may be said of wounds and chains and imprisonment, both because there is no benefit consequent to such patience as there is to the patience of suffering another to be wounded or imprisoned, as also because a man cannot tell, when he sees men proceed against him by violence, whether they intend his death or not. And, lastly, the motive and end for which this renouncing and transferring of right is introduced is nothing else but the security of a man's person in his life and in the means of so preserving life as not to be weary of it. And therefore if a man by words or other signs seem to despoil himself of the end for which those signs were intended, he is not to be understood as if he meant it or that it was his will, but that he was ignorant of how such words and actions were to be interpreted.

The mutual transferring of right is that which men call CONTRACT. There is difference between transferring of right to the thing and transferring, or tradition—that is, delivery—of the thing itself. For the thing may be delivered together with the translation of the right, as in buying and selling with ready money or exchange of goods or lands, and it may be delivered some time after. Again, one of the contractors may deliver the thing contracted for on his part and leave the other to perform his part at some determinate time after and in the meantime be trusted, and then the contract on his part is called PACT OR COVENANT; or both parts may contract now to perform hereafter, in which cases he that is to perform in time to come, being trusted, his performance is called *keeping of promise* or faith, and the failing of performance, if it be voluntary, *violation of faith.* When the transferring of right is not mutual, but one of the parties transfers in hope to gain thereby friendship or service from another or from his friends, or in hope to gain the reputation of charity or magnanimity, or to deliver his mind from the pain of compassion, or in hope of reward in heaven—this is not contract but GIFT, FREE GIFT, GRACE, which words signify one and the same thing.

Signs of contract are either *express* or *by inference.* Express are words spoken with understanding of what they signify, and such words are either of the time *present* or *past*—as *I give, I grant, I have given, I have granted, I will that this be yours*—or of the future—as *I will give, I will grant*—which words of the future are called PROMISE. Signs by inference are sometimes the consequence of words, sometimes the consequence of silence, sometimes the consequence of actions, sometimes the consequence of forbearing an action; and generally a sign by inference of any contract is whatsoever sufficiently argues the will of the contractor. Words alone, if they be of the time to come and contain a bare promise, are an insufficient sign of a free gift and therefore not obligatory. For if they be of the time to come, as *tomorrow I will give,* they are a sign I have not given yet and consequently that my right is not transferred but remains till I transfer it by some other act. But if the words be of the time present or past, as *I have given* or *do give to be delivered tomorrow,* then is my tomorrow's right given away today, and that by the virtue of the words though there were no other argument of my will. And there is a great difference in the signification of these words: *volo hoc tuum esse cras* and *cras dabo*—that is, between *I will that this be yours tomorrow* and *I will give it you tomorrow*—for the word *I will,* in the former manner of speech, signifies an act of the will present, but in the latter it signifies a promise of an act of the will to come; and therefore the former words, being of the present, transfer a future right; the latter, that be of the future, transfer nothing. But if there be other signs of the will to transfer a right besides words, then, though the gift be free, yet may the right be understood to pass by words of the future: as if a man propound a prize to him that comes first to the end of a race, the gift is free; and though the words be of the future, yet the right passes; for if he would not have his words so be understood, he should not have let them run.

In contracts, the right passes not only where the words are of the time present or past but also where they are of the future, because all contract is mutual translation or change of right, and therefore he that promises only because he has already received the benefit for which he promises is to be understood as if he intended the right should pass; for unless he had been content to have his words so understood, the other would not have performed his part first. And for that cause, in buying and selling and other acts of contract a promise is equivalent to a covenant and therefore obligatory.

He that performs first in the case of a contract is said to MERIT that which he is to receive by the performance of the other; and he has it as *due*. Also when a prize is propounded to many which is to be given to him only that wins, or money is thrown among many to be enjoyed by them that catch it, though this be a free gift, yet so to win or so to catch is to *merit* and to have it as DUE. For the right is transferred in the propounding of the prize and in throwing down the money, though it be not determined to whom but by the event of the contention. But there is between these two sorts of merit this difference: that in contract I merit by virtue of my own power and the contractor's need, but in this case of free gift I am enabled to merit only by the benignity of the giver; in contract I merit at the contractor's hand that he should depart with his right, in this case of gift I merit not that the giver should part with his right but that when he has parted with it, it should be mine rather than another's. And this I think to be the meaning of that distinction of the Schools between *meritum congrui* and *meritum condigni*. For God Almighty having promised Paradise to those men, hoodwinked with carnal desires, that can walk through this world according to the precepts and limits prescribed by him, they say he that shall so walk shall merit Paradise *ex congruo*. But because no man can demand a right to it, by his own righteousness or any other power in himself, but by the free grace of God only, they say no man can merit Paradise *ex condigno*.

This, I say, I think is the meaning of that distinction; but because disputers do not agree upon the signification of their own terms of art longer than it serves their turn, I will not affirm anything of their meaning; only this I say: when a gift is given indefinitely, as a prize to be contended for, he that wins merits and may claim the prize as due.

If a covenant be made wherein neither of the parties perform presently but trust one another, in the condition of mere nature, which is a condition of war of every man against every man, upon any reasonable suspicion, it is void; but if there be a common power set over them both, with right and force sufficient to compel performance, it is not void. For he that performs first has no assurance the other will perform after, because the bonds of words are too weak to bridle men's ambition, avarice, anger, and other passions without the fear of some coercive power which in the condition of mere nature, where all men are equal and judges of the justness of their own fears, cannot possibly be supposed. And therefore he which performs first does but betray himself to his enemy, contrary to the right he can never abandon of defending his life and means of living. But in a civil estate, where there is a power set up to constrain those that would otherwise violate their faith, that fear is no more reasonable; and for that cause, he which by the covenant is to perform first is obliged so to do. The cause of fear which makes such a covenant invalid must be always something arising after the covenant made, as some new fact or other sign of the will not to perform; else it cannot make the covenant void. For that which could not hinder a man from promising ought not to be admitted as a hindrance of performing.

He that transfers any right transfers the means of enjoying it, as far as lies in his power. As he that sells land is understood to transfer the herbage and whatsoever grows upon it; nor can he that sells a mill turn away the stream that drives it. And they that give to a man the right of government in sovereignty are understood to give him the right of levying money to maintain soldiers and of appointing magistrates for the administration of justice. . . . The matter or subject of a covenant is always something that falls under deliberation, for to covenant is an act of the will—that is to say, an act, and the last act, of deliberation—and is therefore always understood to be something to come, and which is judged possible for him that covenants to perform.

And therefore to promise that which is known to be impossible is no covenant. But if that prove impossible afterwards which before was thought possible, the covenant is valid, and binds, though not to the thing itself, yet to the value, or, if that also be impossible, to the unfeigned endeavor of performing as much as is possible, for to more no man can be obliged.

Men are freed of their covenants two ways: by performing or by being forgiven. For performance is the natural end of obligation, and forgiveness the restitution of liberty, as being a retransferring of that right in which the obligation consisted. Covenants entered into by fear, in the condition of mere nature, are obligatory. For example, if I covenant to pay a ransom or service for my life to an enemy, I am bound by it; for it is a contract, wherein one receives the benefit of life, the other is to receive money or service for it; and consequently, where no other law, as in the condition of mere nature, forbids the performance, the covenant is valid. Therefore prisoners of war, if trusted with the payment of their ransom, are obliged to pay it; and if a weaker prince make a disadvantageous peace with a stronger, for fear, he is bound to keep it; unless, as has been said before, there arises some new and just cause of fear to renew the war. And even in commonwealths, if I be forced to redeem myself from a thief by promising him money, I am bound to pay it till the civil law discharge me. For whatsoever I may lawfully do without obligation, the same I may lawfully covenant to do through fear; and what I lawfully covenant, I cannot lawfully break. A former covenant makes void a later. For a man that has passed away his right to one man today has it not to pass tomorrow to another; and therefore the later promise passes no right, but is null.

. . . .

From that law of nature by which we are obliged to transfer to another such rights as, being retained, hinder the peace of mankind, there follows a third, which is this: [III] *that men perform their covenants made;* without which covenants are in vain and but empty words, and, the right of all men to all things remaining, we are still in the condition of war. And in this law of nature consists the fountain and original of JUSTICE. For where no covenant has preceded there has no right been transferred, and every man has right to every thing; and consequently no action can be unjust.

But when a covenant is made, then to break it is *unjust;* and the definition of INJUSTICE is no other than *the not performance of covenant.* And whatsoever is not unjust is *just.*

But because covenants of mutual trust, where there is a fear of not performance on either part, as has been said in the former chapter, are invalid, though the original of justice be the making of covenants, yet injustice actually there can be none till the cause of such fear be taken away, which, while men are in the natural condition of war, cannot be done. Therefore, before the names of just and unjust can have place, there must be some coercive power to compel men equally to the performance of their covenants by the terror of some punishment greater than the benefit they expect by the breach of their covenant, and to make good that propriety which by mutual contract men acquire in recompense of the universal right they abandon; and such power there is none before the erection of a commonwealth. And this is also to be gathered out of the ordinary definition of justice in the Schools, for they say that *justice is the constant will of giving to every man his own.* And therefore where there is no *own*—that is, no propriety—there is no injustice; and where there is no coercive power erected—that is, where there is no commonwealth—there is no propriety, all men having right to all things; therefore, where there is no commonwealth, there nothing is unjust. So that the nature of justice consists in keeping of valid covenants; but the validity of covenants begins not but with the constitution of a civil power sufficient to compel men to keep them; and then it is also that propriety begins.

The fool hath said in his heart, there is no such thing as justice; and sometimes also with his tongue, seriously alleging that, every man's conservation and contentment being committed to his own care, there could be no reason why every man might not do what he thought conduced thereunto; and therefore also to make or not make, keep or not keep covenants was not against reason when it conduced to one's benefit. He does not therein deny that there be covenants and that they are sometimes broken, sometimes kept, and that such breach of them may be called injustice and the observance of them justice; but he questions whether injustice, taking away the fear of God—for the same fool hath said in his heart there is no God—may not sometimes stand with that reason which dictates to every man his own good, and particularly then when it conduces to such a benefit as shall put a man in a condition to neglect not only the dispraise and revilings, but also the power of other men. The kingdom of God is gotten by violence; but what if it could be gotten by unjust violence? Were it against reason so to get it, when it is impossible to receive hurt by it? And if it be not against reason, it is not against justice, or else justice is not to be approved for good. From such reasoning as this, successful wickedness has obtained the name of virtue; and some that in all other things have disallowed the violation of faith yet have allowed it when it is for the getting of a kingdom. And the heathen that believed that Saturn was deposed by his son Jupiter believed nevertheless the same Jupiter to be the avenger of injustice—somewhat like to a piece of law in Coke's *Commentaries on Littleton* where he says: if the right heir of the crown be attained of treason, yet the crown shall descend to him and *eo instante* the attainder be void; from which instances a man will be very prone to infer that when the heir apparent of a kingdom shall kill him that is in possession, though his father, you may call it injustice or by what other name you will, yet it can never be against reason, seeing all the voluntary actions of men tend to the benefit of themselves, and those actions are most reasonable that conduce most to their ends. This specious reasoning is nevertheless false.

For the question is not of promises mutual where there is no security of performance on either side—as when there is no civil power erected over the parties promising—for such promises are no covenants; but either where one of the parties has performed already or where there is a power to make him perform, there is the question whether it be against reason—that is, against the benefit of the other—to perform or not. And I say it is not against reason. For the manifestation whereof we are to consider, first, that when a man does a thing which, notwithstanding anything can be foreseen and reckoned on, tends to his own destruction, howsoever some accident which he could not expect, arriving, may turn it to his benefit, yet such events do not make it reasonably or wisely done. Secondly, that in a condition of war, wherein every man to every man, for want of a common power to keep them all in awe, is an enemy, there is no man who can hope by his own strength or wit to defend himself from destruction without the help of confederates, where everyone expects the same defense by the confederation that anyone else does; and therefore he which declares he thinks it reason to deceive those that help him can in reason expect no other means of safety than what can be had from his own single power. He, therefore, that breaks his covenant, and consequently declares that he thinks he may with reason do so, cannot be received into any society that unite themselves for peace and defense, but by the error of them that receive him; nor, when he is received, be retained in it without seeing the danger of their error, which errors a man cannot reasonably reckon upon as the means of his security; and therefore if he be left or cast out of society he perishes, and if he live in society, it is by the errors of other men, which he could not foresee nor reckon upon, and consequently against the reason of his preservation; and so, as all men that contribute not to his destruction, forbear him only out of ignorance of what is good for themselves.

As for the instance of gaining the secure and perpetual felicity of heaven by any way, it is frivolous, there being but one way imaginable, and that is not breaking but keeping of covenant.

And for the other instance of attaining sovereignty by rebellion, it is manifest that, though the event follow, yet because it cannot reasonably be expected, but rather the contrary, and because by gaining it so others are taught to gain the same in like manner, the attempt thereof is against reason. Justice, therefore—that is to say, keeping of covenant—is a rule of reason by which we are forbidden to do anything destructive to our life, and consequently a law of nature.

There be some that proceed further and will not have the law of nature to be those rules which conduce to the preservation of man's life on earth but to the attaining of an eternal felicity after death, to which they think the breach of covenant may conduce and consequently be just and reasonable; such are they that think it a work of merit to kill or depose or rebel against the sovereign power constituted over them by their own consent. But because there is no natural knowledge of man's estate after death—much less of the reward that is then to be given to breach of faith—but only a belief grounded upon other men's saying that they know it supernaturally, or that they know those that knew them that knew others that knew it supernaturally, breach of faith cannot be called a precept of reason or nature.

Others that allow for a law of nature the keeping of faith do nevertheless make exception of certain persons, as heretics and such as use not to perform their covenant to others; and this also is against reason. For if any fault of a man be sufficient to discharge our covenant made, the same ought in reason to have been sufficient to have hindered the making of it.

The names of just and unjust, when they are attributed to men, signify one thing, and when they are attributed to actions, another. When they are attributed to men, they signify conformity or inconformity of manners to reason. But when they are attributed to actions, they signify the conformity or inconformity to reason, not of manners or manner of life, but of particular actions. A just man, therefore, is he that takes all the care he can that his actions may be all just; and an unjust man is he that neglects it. And such men are more often in our language styled by the names of righteous and unrighteous than just and unjust, though the meaning be the same. Therefore a righteous man does not lose that title by one or a few unjust actions that proceed from sudden passion or mistake of things or persons; nor does an unrighteous man lose his character for such action as he does or forbears to do for fear, because his will is not framed by the justice but by the apparent benefit of what he is to do. That which gives to human actions the relish of justice is a certain nobleness or gallantness of courage, rarely found, by which a man scorns to be beholden for the contentment of his life to fraud or breach of promise. This justice of the manners is that which is meant where justice is called a virtue and injustice a vice. But the justice of actions denominates men, not just, but *guiltless;* and the injustice of the same, which is also called injury, gives them but the name of *guilty*.

Again, the injustice of manners is the disposition or aptitude to do injury, and is injustice before it proceed to act and without supposing any individual person injured. But the injustice of an action—that is to say, injury—supposes an individual person injured—namely, him to whom the covenant was made—and therefore many times the injury is received by one man when the damage redounds to another. As when the master commands his servant to give money to a stranger: if it be not done, the injury is done to the master, whom he had before covenanted to obey; but the damage redounds to the stranger, to whom he had no obligation and therefore could not injure him. And so also in commonwealths private men may remit to one another their debts but not robberies or other violences whereby they are endamaged; because the detaining of debts is an injury to themselves, but robbery and violence are injuries to the person of the commonwealth.

Whatsoever is done to a man, conformable to his own will signified to the doer, is no injury to him. For if he that does it has not passed away his original right to do what he please by some antecedent covenant, there is no breach of covenant and therefore no injury done him. And if he have, then his will to have it done, being signified, is a release of that covenant, and so again there is no injury done him.

Justice of actions is by writers divided into *commutative* and *distributive;* and the former they say consists in proportion arithmetical, the latter in proportion geometrical. Commutative, therefore, they place in the equality of value of the things contracted for, and distributive in the distribution of equal benefit to men of equal merit. As if it were injustice to sell dearer than we buy, or to give more to a man than he merits. The value of all things contracted for is measured by the appetite of the contractors, and therefore the just value is that which they be contented to give. And merit (besides that which is by covenant, where the performance on one part merits the performance of the other part, and falls under justice commutative, not distributive) is not due by justice, but is rewarded of grace only. And therefore this distinction, in the sense wherein it uses to be expounded, is not right. To speak properly, commutative justice is the justice of a contractor—that is, a performance of covenant in buying and selling, hiring and letting to hire, lending and borrowing, exchanging, bartering, and other acts of contract. And distributive justice, the justice of an arbitrator—that is to say, the act of defining what is just. Wherein, being trusted by them that make him arbitrator, if he perform his trust, he is said to distribute to every man his own; and this is indeed just distribution, and may be called, though improperly, distributive justice, but more properly equity, which also is a law of nature, as shall be shown in due place.

As justice depends on antecedent covenant, so does GRATITUDE depend on antecedent grace—that is to say, antecedent free gift—and is the fourth law of nature, which may be conceived in this form: [IV] *that a man which receives benefit from another of mere grace endeavor that he which gives it have no reasonable cause to repent him of his good will.* For no man gives but with intention of good to himself, because gift is voluntary, and of all voluntary acts the object is to every man his own good; of which if men see they shall be frustrated, there will be no beginning of benevolence or trust nor consequently of mutual help nor of reconciliation of one man to another; and therefore they are to remain still in the condition of *war,* which is contrary to the first and fundamental law of nature, which commands men to *seek peace.* The breach of this law is called *ingratitude,* and has the same relation to grace that injustice has to obligation by covenant.

A fifth law of nature is COMPLAISANCE—that is to say, [V] *that every man strive to accommodate himself to the rest.* For the understanding whereof we may consider that there is in men's aptness to society a diversity of nature rising from their diversity of affections not unlike to that we see in stones brought together for building of an edifice. For as that stone which by the asperity and irregularity of figure takes more room from others than itself fills, and for the hardness cannot be easily made plain and thereby hinders the building, is by the builders cast away as unprofitable and troublesome, so also a man that by asperity of nature will strive to retain those things which to himself are superfluous and to others necessary, and for the stubbornness of his passions cannot be corrected, is to be left or cast out of society as cumbersome thereunto. For seeing every man, not only by right but also by necessity of nature, is supposed to endeavor all he can to obtain that which is necessary for his conservation, he that shall oppose himself against it for things superfluous is guilty of the war that thereupon is to follow, and therefore does that which is contrary to the fundamental law of nature, which commands *to seek peace.* The observers of this law may be called SOCIABLE (the Latins call them *commodi*), the contrary *stubborn, insociable, forward, intractable.*

A sixth law of nature is this: [VI] *that upon caution of the future time, a man ought to pardon the offenses past of them that, repenting, desire it.* For PARDON is nothing but granting of peace, which, though granted to them that persevere in their hostility, be not peace but fear, yet, not granted to them that give caution of the future time, is sign of an aversion to peace, and therefore contrary to the law of nature.

A seventh is [VII] *that in revenges*—that is, retribution of evil for evil—*men look not at the greatness of the evil past, but the greatness of the good to follow.* Whereby we are forbidden to inflict punishment with any other design than for correction of the offender or direction of others. For this law is consequent to the next before it that commands pardon upon security of the future time. Besides, revenge without respect to the example and profit to come is a triumph or glorying in the hurt of another, tending to no end; for the end is always somewhat to come, and glorying to no end is vainglory and contrary to reason; and to hurt without reason tends to the introduction of war, which is against the law of nature and is commonly styled by the name of *cruelty.*

And because all signs of hatred or contempt provoke to fight, insomuch as most men choose rather to hazard their life than not to be revenged, we may in the eighth place for a law of nature set down this precept: [VIII] *that no man by deed, word, countenance, or gesture declare hatred or contempt of another.* The breach of which law is commonly called *contumely.*

The question who is the better man has no place in the condition of mere nature, where, as has been shown before, all men are equal. The inequality that now is has been introduced by the laws civil. I know that Aristotle in the first book of his *Politics,* for a foundation of his doctrine, makes men by nature some more worthy to command, meaning the wiser sort such as he thought himself to be for his philosophy, others to serve, meaning those that had strong bodies but were not philosophers as he; as if master and servant were not introduced by consent of men but by difference of wit, which is not only against reason but also against experience. For there are very few so foolish that had not rather govern themselves than be governed by others; nor when the wise in their own conceit contend by force with them who distrust their own wisdom, do they always, or often, or almost at any time, get the victory. If nature therefore have made men equal, that equality is to be acknowledged; or if nature have made men unequally, yet because men that think themselves equal will not enter into conditions of peace but upon equal terms, such equality must be admitted. And therefore for the ninth law of nature, I put this: [IX] *that every man acknowledge another for his equal by nature.* The breach of this precept is *pride.*

On this law depends another: [X] *that at the entrance into conditions of peace, no man require to reserve to himself any right which he is not content should be reserved to every one of the rest.* As it is necessary for all men that seek peace to lay down certain rights of nature—that is to say, not to have liberty to do all they list—so is it necessary for man's life to retain some, as right to govern their own bodies, enjoy air, water, motion, ways to go from place to place, and all things else without which a man cannot live or not live well. If in this case, at the making of peace, men require for themselves that which they would not have to be granted to others, they do contrary to the precedent law that commands the acknowledgment of natural equality and therefore also the law of nature. The observers of this law are those we call *modest,* and the breakers *arrogant* men. The Greeks call the violation of this law πλεονεξία—that is, a desire of more than their share.

Also if *a man be trusted to judge between man and man,* it is a precept of the law of nature [XI] *that he deal equally between them.* For without that, the controversies of men cannot be determined but by war. He, therefore, that is partial in judgment does what in him lies to deter men from the use of judges and arbitrators, and consequently, against the fundamental law of nature, is the cause of war. The observance of this law, from the equal distribution to each man of that which in reason belongs to him, is called EQUITY and, as I have said before, distributive justice; the violation, *acception of persons,* προσωποληψία.

And from this follows another law: [XII] *that such things as cannot be divided be enjoyed in common, if it can be; and if the quantity of the thing permit, without stint; otherwise proportionably to the number of them that have right.* For otherwise the distribution is unequal and contrary to equity.

But some things there be that can neither be divided nor enjoyed in common. Then the law of nature, which prescribes equity, requires [XIII] *that the entire right, or else—making the use alternate—the first possession, be determined by lot.* For equal distribution is of the law of nature; and other means of equal distribution cannot be imagined.

Of *lots* there be two sorts: *arbitrary* and *natural.* Arbitrary is that which is agreed on by the competitors; natural is either *primogeniture* (which the Greek calls κληρονομία, which signifies *given by lot*) or *first seizure.* And therefore [XIV] those things which cannot be enjoyed in common, nor divided, ought to be adjudged to the first possessor; and in some cases to the first-born, as acquired by lot.

It is also a law of nature [XV] *that all men that mediate peace be allowed safe conduct.* For the law that commands peace, as the *end,* commands intercession, as the *means;* and to intercession the means is safe conduct.

And because, though men be never so willing to observe these laws, there may nevertheless arise questions concerning a man's action—first, whether it were done or not done; secondly, if done, whether against the law or not against the law; the former whereof is called a question *of fact,* the latter a question *of right*—therefore, unless the parties to the question covenant mutually to stand to the sentence of another, they are as far from peace as ever. This other to whose sentence they submit is called an ARBITRATOR. And therefore it is of the law of nature [XVI] *that they that are at controversy submit their right to the judgment of an arbitrator.*

And seeing every man is presumed to do all things in order to his own benefit, [XVII] no man is a fit arbitrator in his own cause; and if he were never so fit, yet, equity allowing to each party equal benefit, if one be admitted to be judge the other is to be admitted also; and so the controversy—that is, the cause of war—remains against the law of nature.

For the same reason [XVIII] no man in any cause ought to be received for arbitrator to whom greater profit or honor or pleasure apparently arises out of the victory of one party than of the other; for he has taken, though an unavoidable bribe, yet a bribe, and no man can be obliged to trust him. And thus also the controversy and the condition of war remains, contrary to the law of nature.

And [XIX] in a controversy of *fact,* the judge being to give no more credit to one than to the other, if there be no other arguments, must give credit to a third, or to a third and fourth, no more; for else the question is undecided and left to force, contrary to the law of nature.

These are the laws of nature dictating peace for a means of the conservation of men in multitudes, and which only concern the doctrine of civil society. There be other things tending to the destruction of particular men—as drunkenness and all other parts of intemperance—which may therefore also be reckoned among those things which the law of nature has forbidden, but are not necessary to be mentioned nor are pertinent enough to this place. And though this may seem too subtle a deduction of the laws of nature to be taken notice of by all men—whereof the most part are too busy in getting food and the rest too negligent to understand—

yet to leave all men inexcusable they have been contracted into one easy sum, intelligible even to the meanest capacity, and that is *Do not that to another which you would not have done to yourself;* which shows him that he has no more to do in learning the laws of nature but, when weighing the actions of other men with his own they seem too heavy, to put them into the other part of the balance and his own into their place, that his own passions and self-love may add nothing to the weight, and then there is none of these laws of nature that will not appear unto him very reasonable.

. . . .

JOHN STUART MILL

On the Connection between Justice and Utility

In all ages of speculation one of the strongest obstacles to the reception of the doctrine that utility or happiness is the criterion of right and wrong has been drawn from the idea of justice. The powerful sentiment and apparently clear perception which that word recalls with a rapidity and certainty resembling an instinct have seemed to the majority of thinkers to point to an inherent quality in things; to show that the just must have an existence in nature as something absolute, generically distinct from every variety of the expedient and, in idea, opposed to it, though (as is commonly acknowledged) never, in the long run, disjointed from it in fact.

In the case of this, as of our other moral sentiments, there is no necessary connection between the question of its origin and that of its binding force. That a feeling is bestowed on us by nature does not necessarily legitimate all its promptings. The feeling of justice might be a peculiar instinct, and might yet require, like our other instincts, to be controlled and enlightened by a higher reason. If we have intellectual instincts leading us to judge in a particular way, as well as animal instincts that prompt us to act in a particular way, there is no necessity that the former should be more infallible in their sphere than the latter in theirs; it may as well happen that wrong judgments are occasionally suggested by those, as wrong actions by these. But though it is one thing to believe that we have natural feelings of justice, and another to

From *Utilitarianism,* ch. 5 (1861). The notes are Mill's own.

acknowledge them as an ultimate criterion of conduct, these two opinions are very closely connected in point of fact. Mankind are always predisposed to believe that any subjective feeling, not otherwise accounted for, is a revelation of some objective reality. Our present object is to determine whether the reality to which the feeling of justice corresponds is one which needs any such special revelation, whether the justice or injustice of an action is a thing intrinsically peculiar and distinct from all its other qualities or only a combination of certain of those qualities presented under a peculiar aspect. For the purpose of this inquiry it is practically important to consider whether the feeling itself, of justice and injustice, is *sui generis* like our sensations of color and taste or a derivative feeling formed by a combination of others. And this it is the more essential to examine, as people are in general willing enough to allow that objectively the dictates of justice coincide with a part of the field of general expediency; but inasmuch as the subjective mental feeling of justice is different from that which commonly attaches to simple expediency, and, except in the extreme cases of the latter, is far more imperative in its demands, people find it difficult to see in justice only a particular kind or branch of general utility, and think that its superior binding force requires a totally different origin.

To throw light upon this question, it is necessary to attempt to ascertain what is the distinguishing character of justice, or of injustice; what is the quality, or whether there is any quality, attributed in common to all modes of conduct designated as unjust (for justice, like many other moral attributes, is best defined by its opposite), and distinguishing them from such modes of conduct as are disapproved, but without having that particular epithet of disapprobation applied to them. If in everything which men are accustomed to characterize as just or unjust some one common attribute or collection of attributes is always present, we may judge whether this particular attribute or combination of attributes would be capable of gathering round it a sentiment of that peculiar character and intensity by virtue of the general laws of our emotional constitution, or whether the sentiment is inexplicable and requires to be regarded as a special provision of nature. If we find the former to be the case, we shall, in resolving this question, have resolved also the main problem; if the latter, we shall have to seek for some other mode of investigating it.

To find the common attributes of a variety of objects, it is necessary to begin by surveying the objects themselves in the concrete. Let us therefore advert successively to the various modes of action and arrangements of human affairs which are classed, by universal or widely spread opinion, as just or as unjust. The things well known to excite the sentiments associated with those names are of a very multifarious character. I shall pass them rapidly in review, without studying any particular arrangement.

In the first place, it is mostly considered unjust to deprive anyone of his personal liberty, his property, or any other thing which belongs to him by law. Here, therefore, is one instance of the application of the terms "just" and "unjust" in a perfectly definite sense, namely, that it is just to respect, unjust to violate, the *legal rights* of anyone. But this judgment admits of several exceptions, arising from the other forms in which the notions of justice and injustice present themselves. For example, the person who suffers the deprivation may (as the phrase is) have *forfeited* the rights which he is so deprived of—a case to which we shall return presently. But also—

Secondly, the legal rights of which he is deprived may be rights which *ought* not to have belonged to him; in other words, the law which confers on him these rights may be a bad law. When it is so or when (which is the same thing for our purpose) it is supposed to be so, opinions will differ as to the justice or injustice of infringing it. Some maintain that no law, however bad, ought to be disobeyed by an individual citizen; that his opposition to it, if shown at all, should only be shown in endeavoring to get it altered by competent authority. This opinion (which condemns many of the most illustrious benefactors of mankind, and would often protect pernicious institutions against the only weapons which, in the state of things existing at the time, have any chance of succeeding against them) is defended by those who hold it on grounds of expediency, principally on that of the importance to the common interest of mankind, of maintaining inviolate the sentiment of submission to law. Other persons, again, hold the directly contrary opinion that any law, judged to be bad, may blamelessly be disobeyed, even though it be not judged to be unjust but only inexpedient, while others would confine the license of disobedience to the case of unjust laws; but, again, some say that all laws which are inexpedient are unjust, since every law imposes some restriction on the natural liberty of mankind, which restriction is an injustice unless legitimated by tending to their good. Among these diversities of opinion it seems to be universally admitted that there may be unjust laws, and that law, consequently, is not the ultimate criterion of justice, but may give to one person a benefit, or impose on another an evil, which justice condemns. When, however, a law is thought to be unjust, it seems always to be regarded as being so in the same way in which a breach of law is unjust, namely, by infringing somebody's right, which, as it cannot in this case be a legal right, receives a different appellation and is called a moral right. We may say, therefore, that a second case of injustice consists in taking or withholding from any person that to which he has a *moral right.*

Thirdly, it is universally considered just that each person should obtain that (whether good or evil) which he *deserves,* and unjust that he should obtain a good or be made to undergo an evil which he does not deserve. This is, perhaps, the clearest and most emphatic form in which the idea of justice is conceived by the general mind. As it involves the notion of desert, the question arises what constitutes desert? Speaking in a general way, a person is understood to deserve good if he does right, evil if he does wrong; and in a more particular sense, to deserve good from those to whom he does or has done good, and evil from those to whom he does or has done evil. The precept of returning good for evil has never been regarded as a case of the fulfillment of justice, but as one in which the claims of justice are waived, in obedience to other considerations.

Fourthly, it is confessedly unjust to *break faith* with anyone: to violate an engagement, either express or implied, or disappoint expectations raised by our own conduct, at least if we have raised those expectations knowingly and voluntarily. Like the other obligations of justice already spoken of, this one is not regarded as absolute, but as capable of being overruled by a stronger obligation of justice on the other side, or by such conduct on the part of the person concerned as is deemed to absolve us from our obligation to him and to constitute a *forfeiture* of the benefit which he has been led to expect.

Fifthly, it is, by universal admission, inconsistent with justice to be *partial*—to show favor or preference to one person over another in matters to which favor and preference do not properly apply. Impartiality, however, does not seem to be regarded as a duty in itself, but rather as instrumental to some other duty; for it is admitted that favor and preference are not always censurable, and, indeed, the cases in which they are condemned are rather the exception than the rule. A person would be more likely to be blamed than applauded for giving his family or friends no superiority in good offices over strangers when he could do so without violating any other duty; and no one thinks it unjust to seek one person in preference to another as a friend, connection, or companion. Impartiality where rights are concerned is of course obligatory, but this is involved in the more general obligation of giving to everyone his right. A tribunal, for example, must be impartial because it is bound to award, without regard to any other consideration, a disputed object to the one of two parties who has the right to it. There are other cases in which impartiality means being solely influenced by desert, as with those who, in the capacity of judges, preceptors, or parents, administer reward and punishment as such. There are cases, again, in which it means being solely influenced by consideration for the public interest, as in making a selection among candidates for a government employment. Impartiality, in short, as an obligation of justice, may be said to mean being exclusively influenced by the considerations which it is supposed ought to influence the particular case in hand, and resisting solicitation of any motives which prompt to conduct different from what those considerations would dictate.

Nearly allied to the idea of impartiality is that of *equality,* which often enters as a component part both into the conception of justice and into the practice of it, and, in the eyes of many persons, constitutes its essence. But in this, still more than in any other case, the notion of justice varies in different persons, and always conforms in its variations to their notion of utility. Each person maintains that equality is the dictate of justice, except where he thinks that expediency requires inequality. The justice of giving equal protection to the rights of all is maintained by those who support the most outrageous inequality in the rights themselves. Even in slave countries it is theoretically admitted that the rights of the slave, such as they are, ought to be as sacred as those of the master, and that a tribunal which fails to enforce them with equal strictness is wanting in justice; while, at the same time, institutions which leave to the slave scarcely any rights to enforce are not deemed unjust because they are not deemed inexpedient. Those who think that utility requires distinctions of rank do not consider it unjust that riches and social privileges should be unequally dispensed; but those who think this inequality inexpedient think it unjust also. Whoever thinks that government is necessary sees no injustice in as much inequality as is constituted by giving to the magistrate powers not granted to other people. Even among those who hold leveling doctrines, there are differences of opinion about expediency. Some communists consider it unjust that the produce of the labor of the community should be shared on any other principle than that of exact equality; others think it just that those should receive most whose wants are greatest; while others hold that those who work harder, or who produce more, or whose services are more valuable to the community, may justly claim a larger quota in the division of the produce. And the sense of natural justice may be plausibly appealed to in behalf of every one of these opinions.

Among so many diverse applications of the term "justice," which yet is not regarded as ambiguous, it is a matter of some difficulty to seize the mental link which holds them together, and on which the moral sentiment adhering to the term essentially depends. Perhaps, in this embarrassment, some help may be derived from the history of the word, as indicated by its etymology.

In most if not in all languages, the etymology of the word which corresponds to "just" points distinctly to an origin connected with the ordinances of law. *Justum* is a form of *jussum,* that which has been ordered. *Dikaion* comes directly from *dike,* a suit at law. *Recht,* from which came *right* and *righteous,* is synonymous with law. The courts of justice, the administration of justice, are the courts and the administration of law. *La justice,* in French, is the established term for judicature. I am not committing the fallacy, imputed with some show of truth to Horne Tooke, of assuming that a word must still continue to mean what it originally meant. Etymology is slight evidence of what the idea now signified is, but the very best evidence of how it sprang up. There can, I think, be no doubt that the *idée mère,* the primitive element, in the formation of the notion of justice was conformity to law. It constituted the entire idea among the Hebrews up to the birth of Christianity; as might be expected in the case of a people whose laws attempted to embrace all subjects on which precepts were required, and who believed those laws to be a direct emanation from the Supreme

Being. But other nations, and in particular the Greeks and Romans, who knew that their laws had been made originally, and still continued to be made, by men, were not afraid to admit that those men might make bad laws; might do, by law, the same things, and from the same motives, which if done by individuals without the sanction of law would be called unjust. And hence the sentiment of injustice came to be attached, not to all violations of law, but only to violations of such laws as *ought* to exist, including such as ought to exist but do not, and to laws themselves if supposed to be contrary to what ought to be law. In this manner the idea of law and of its injunctions was still predominant in the notion of justice, even when the laws actually in force ceased to be accepted as the standard of it.

It is true that mankind consider the idea of justice and its obligations as applicable to many things which neither are, nor is it desired that they should be, regulated by law. Nobody desires that laws should interfere with the whole detail of private life; yet everyone allows that in all daily conduct a person may and does show himself to be either just or unjust. But even here, the idea of the breach of what ought to be law still lingers in a modified shape. It would always give us pleasure, and chime in with our feelings of fitness, that acts which we deem unjust should be punished, though we do not always think it expedient that this should be done by the tribunals. We forego that gratification on account of incidental inconveniences. We should be glad to see just conduct enforced and injustice repressed, even in the minutest details, if we were not, with reason, afraid of trusting the magistrate with so unlimited an amount of power over individuals. When we think that a person is bound in justice to do a thing, it is an ordinary form of language to say that he ought to be compelled to do it. We should be gratified to see the obligation enforced by anybody who had the power. If we see that its enforcement by law would be inexpedient, we lament the impossibility, we consider the impunity given to injustice as an evil, and strive to make amends for it by bringing a strong expression of our own and the public disapprobation to bear upon the offender. Thus the idea of legal constraint is still the generating idea of the notion of justice, though undergoing several tranformations before that notion as it exists in an advanced state of society becomes complete.

The above is, I think, a true account, as far as it goes, of the origin and progressive growth of the idea of justice. But we must observe that it contains as yet nothing to distinguish that obligation from moral obligation in general. For the truth is that the idea of penal sanction, which is the essence of law, enters not only into the conception of injustice, but into that of any kind of wrong. We do not call anything wrong unless we mean to imply that a person ought to be punished in some way or other for doing it—if not by law, by the opinion of his fellow creatures; if not by opinion, by the reproaches of his own conscience. This seems the real turning point of the distinction between morality and simple expediency. It is a part of the notion of duty in every one of its forms that a person may rightfully be compelled to fulfill it. Duty is a thing which may be *exacted* from a person, as one exacts a debt. Unless we think that it may be exacted from him, we do not call it his duty. Reasons of prudence, or the interest of other people, may militate against actually exacting it, but the person himself, it is clearly understood, would not be entitled to complain. There are other things, on the contrary, which we wish that people should do, which we like or admire them for doing, perhaps dislike or despise them for not doing, but yet admit that they are not bound to do; it is not a case of moral obligation; we do not blame them, that is, we do not think that they are proper objects of punishment. How we come by these ideas of deserving and not deserving punishment will appear, perhaps, in the sequel; but I think there is no doubt that this distinction lies at the bottom of the notions of right and wrong; that we call any conduct wrong, or employ, instead, some other term of dislike or disparagement, according as we think that the person ought, or ought not, to be punished for it; and we say it would be right to do so and so, or merely that it would be desirable or laudable, according as we would wish to see the person whom it concerns compelled, or only persuaded and exhorted, to act in that manner.[1]

This, therefore, being the characteristic difference which marks off, not justice, but morality in general from the remaining provinces of expediency and worthiness, the character is still to be sought which distinguishes justice from other branches of morality. Now it is known that ethical writers divide moral duties into two

[1] See this point enforced and illustrated by Professor Bain, in an admirable chapter (entitled "The Ethical Emotions, or the Moral Sense"), of the second of the two treatises composing his elaborate and profound work on the Mind.

classes, denoted by the ill-chosen expressions, duties of perfect and of imperfect obligation; the latter being those in which, though the act is obligatory, the particular occasions of performing it are left to our choice, as in the case of charity or beneficence, which we are indeed bound to practice but not toward any definite person, nor at any prescribed time. In the more precise language of philosophic jurists, duties of perfect obligation are those duties in virtue of which a correlative *right* resides in some person or persons; duties of imperfect obligation are those moral obligations which do not give birth to any right. I think it will be found that this distinction exactly coincides with that which exists between justice and the other obligations of morality. In our survey of the various popular acceptations of justice, the term appeared generally to involve the idea of a personal right—a claim on the part of one or more individuals, like that which the law gives when it confers a proprietary or other legal right. Whether the injustice consists in depriving a person of a possession, or in breaking faith with him, or in treating him worse than he deserves, or worse than other people who have no greater claims—in each case the supposition implies two things: a wrong done, and some assignable person who is wronged. Injustice may also be done by treating a person better than others; but the wrong in this case is to his competitors, who are also assignable persons. It seems to me that this feature in the case—a right in some person, correlative to the moral obligation—constitutes the specific difference between justice and generosity or beneficence. Justice implies something which it is not only right to do, and wrong not to do, but which some individual person can claim from us as his moral right. No one has a moral right to our generosity or beneficence because we are not morally bound to practice those virtues toward any given individual. And it will be found with respect to this as to every correct definition that the instances which seem to conflict with it are those which most confirm it. For if a moralist attempts, as some have done, to make out that mankind generally, though not any given individual, have a right to all the good we can do them, he at once, by that thesis, includes generosity and beneficence within the category of justice. He is obliged to say that our utmost exertions are *due* to our fellow creatures, thus assimilating them to a debt; or that nothing less can be a sufficient *return* for what society does for us, thus classing the case as one of gratitude; both of which are acknowledged cases of justice, and not of the virtue of beneficence; and whoever does not place the distinction between justice and morality in general, where we have now placed it, will be found to make no distinction between them at all, but to merge all morality in justice.

Having thus endeavored to determine the distinctive elements which enter into the composition of the idea of justice, we are ready to enter on the inquiry whether the feeling which accompanies the idea is attached to it by a special dispensation of nature, or whether it could have grown up, by any known laws, out of the idea itself; and, in particular, whether it can have originated in considerations of general expediency.

I conceive that the sentiment itself does not arise from anything which would commonly or correctly be termed an idea of expediency, but that, though the sentiment does not, whatever is moral in it does.

We have seen that the two essential ingredients in the sentiment of justice are the desire to punish a person who has done harm and the knowledge or belief that there is some definite individual or individuals to whom harm has been done.

Now it appears to me that the desire to punish a person who has done harm to some individual is a spontaneous outgrowth from two sentiments, both in the highest degree natural and which either are or resemble instincts: the impulse of self-defense and the feeling of sympathy.

It is natural to resent and to repel or retaliate any harm done or attempted against ourselves or against those with whom we sympathize. The origin of this sentiment it is not necessary here to discuss. Whether it be an instinct or a result of intelligence, it is, we know, common to all animal nature; for every animal tries to hurt those who have hurt, or who it thinks are about to hurt, itself or its young. Human beings, on this point, only differ from other animals in two particulars. First, in being capable of sympathizing, not solely with their offspring, or, like some of the more noble animals, with some superior animal who is kind to them, but with all human, and even with all sentient, beings; secondly, in having a more developed intelligence, which gives a wider range to the whole of their sentiments, whether self-regarding or sympathetic. By virtue of his superior intelligence, even apart from his superior range of sympathy, a human being is capable of apprehending a community of interest between himself and the human society of which he forms a part, such that any conduct which threatens the security of the society generally is threatening to his own, and calls forth his instinct (if instinct it be) of self-defense. The same superiority of intelligence, joined to the power of sympathizing with human beings generally, enables him to attach himself to the collective idea of his tribe, his country, or mankind in such a manner that any act hurtful to them raises his instinct of sympathy and urges him to resistance.

The sentiment of justice, in that one of its elements which consists of the desire to punish, is thus, I conceive, the natural feeling of retaliation or vengeance, rendered by intellect and sympathy applicable to those injuries, that is, to those hurts, which wound us through, or in common with, society at large. This sentiment, in itself, has nothing moral in it; what is moral is the exclusive subordination of it to the social sympathies, so as to wait on and obey their call. For the natural feeling would make us resent indiscriminately whatever anyone does that is disagreeable to us; but, when moralized by the social feeling, it only acts in the directions conformable to the general good: just persons resenting a hurt to society, though not otherwise a hurt to themselves, and not resenting a hurt to themselves, however painful, unless it be of the kind which society has a common interest with them in the repression of.

It is no objection against this doctrine to say that, when we feel our sentiment of justice outraged, we are not thinking of society at large or of any collective interest, but only of the individual case. It is common enough, certainly, though the reverse of commendable, to feel resentment merely because we have suffered pain; but a person whose resentment is really a moral feeling, that is, who considers whether an act is blamable before he allows himself to resent it—such a person, though he may not say expressly to himself that he is standing up for the interest of society, certainly does feel that he is asserting a rule which is for the benefit of others as well as for his own. If he is not feeling this, if he is regarding the act solely as it affects him individually, he is not consciously just; he is not concerning himself about the justice of his actions. This is admitted even by anti-utilitarian moralists. When Kant (as before remarked) propounds as the fundamental principle of morals, "So act that thy rule of conduct might be adopted as a law by all rational beings," he virtually acknowledges that the interest of mankind collectively, or at least of mankind indiscriminately, must be in the mind of the agent when conscientiously deciding on the morality of the act. Otherwise he uses words without a meaning; for that a rule even of utter selfishness could not *possibly* be adopted by all rational beings—that there is any insuperable obstacle in the nature of things to its adoption—cannot be even plausibly maintained. To give any meaning to Kant's principle, the sense put upon it must be that we ought to shape our conduct by a rule which all rational beings might adopt *with benefit to their collective interest.*

To recapitulate: the idea of justice supposes two things—a rule of conduct and a sentiment which sanctions the rule. The first must be supposed common to all mankind and intended for their good. The other (the sentiment) is a desire that punishment may be suffered by those who infringe the rule. There is involved, in addition, the conception of some definite person who suffers by the infringement, whose rights (to use the expression appropriated to the case) are violated by it. And the sentiment of justice appears to me to be the animal desire to repel or retaliate a hurt or damage to oneself or to those with whom one sympathizes, widened so as to include all persons, by the human capacity of enlarged sympathy and the human conception of intelligent self-interest. From the latter elements the feeling derives its morality; from the former, its peculiar impressiveness and energy of self-assertion.

I have, throughout, treated the idea of a *right* residing in the injured person and violated by the injury, not as a separate element in the composition of the idea and sentiment, but as one of the forms in which the other two elements clothe themselves. These elements are a hurt to some assignable person or persons, on the one hand, and a demand for punishment, on the other. An examination of our own minds, I think, will show that these two things include all that we mean when we speak of violation of a right. When we call anything a person's right, we mean that he has a valid claim on society to protect him in the possession of it, either by the force of law or by that of education and opinion. If he has what we consider a sufficient claim, on whatever account, to have something guaranteed to him by society, we say that he has a right to it. If we desire to prove that anything does not belong to him by right, we think this done as soon as it is admitted that society ought not to take measures for securing it to him, but should leave him to chance or to his own exertions. Thus a person is said to have a right to what he can earn in fair professional competition, because society ought not to allow any other person to hinder him from endeavoring to earn in that manner as much as he can. But he has not a right to three hundred a year, though he may happen to be earning it; because society is not called on to provide that he shall earn that sum. On the contrary, if he owns ten thousand pounds three-per-cent stock, he *has* a right to three hundred a year because society has come under an obligation to provide him with an income of that amount.

To have a right, then, is, I conceive, to have something which society ought to defend me in the possession of. If the objector goes on to ask why it ought, I can give him no other reason than general utility. If that expression does not seem to convey a sufficient feeling of the strength of the obligation, nor to account for the peculiar energy of the feeling, it is because there goes to the composition of the sentiment, not a rational only but also an animal element—the thirst for retaliation; and this thirst derives its intensity, as well as its moral justification, from the extraordinarily important and impressive kind of utility which is concerned. The interest involved is that of security, to everyone's feelings the most vital of all interests. All other earthly benefits are needed by one person, not needed by another; and many of them can, if necessary, be cheerfully foregone or replaced by something else; but security no human being can possibly do without; on it we depend for all our immunity from evil and for the whole value of all and every good, beyond the passing moment, since nothing but the gratification of the instant could be of any worth to us if we could be deprived of everything the next instant by whoever was momentarily stronger than ourselves. Now this most indispensable of all necessaries, after physical nutriment, cannot be had unless the machinery for providing it is kept unintermittedly in active play. Our notion, therefore, of the claim we have on our fellow creatures to join in making safe for us the very groundwork of our existence gathers feelings around it so much more intense than those concerned in any of the more common cases of utility that the difference in degree (as is often the case in psychology) becomes a real difference in kind. The claim assumes that character of absoluteness, that apparent infinity and incommensurability with all other considerations which constitute the distinction between the feeling of right and wrong and that of ordinary expediency and inexpediency. The feelings concerned are so powerful, and we count so positively on finding a responsive feeling in others (all being alike interested) that *ought* and *should* grow into *must,* and recognized indispensability becomes a moral necessity, analogous to physical, and often not inferior to it in binding force.

If the preceding analysis, or something resembling it, be not the correct account of the notion of justice—if justice be totally independent of utility, and be a standard *per se,* which the mind can recognize by simple introspection of itself—it is hard to understand why that internal oracle is so ambiguous, and why so many things appear either just or unjust, according to the light in which they are regarded.

We are continually informed that utility is an uncertain standard, which every different person interprets differently, and that there is no safety but in the immutable, ineffaceable, and unmistakable dictates of justice, which carry their evidence in themselves and are independent of the fluctuations of opinion. One would suppose from this that on questions of justice there could be no controversy; that, if we take that for our rule, its application to any given case could leave us in as little doubt as a mathematical demonstration. So far is this from being the fact that there is as much difference of opinion, and as much discussion, about what is just as about what is useful to society. Not only have different nations and individuals different notions of justice, but in the mind of one and the same individual, justice is not some one rule, principle, or maxim, but many which do not always coincide in their dictates, and, in choosing between which, he is guided either by some extraneous standard or by his own personal predilections.

For instance, there are some who say that it is unjust to punish anyone for the sake of example to others, that punishment is just only when intended for the good of the sufferer himself. Others maintain the extreme reverse, contending that to punish persons who have attained years of discretion, for their own benefit, is despotism and injustice, since, if the matter at issue is solely their own good, no one has a right to control their own judgment of it; but that they may justly be punished to prevent evil to others, this being the exercise of the legitimate right of self-defense. Mr. Owen, again, affirms that it is unjust to punish at all, for the criminal did not make his own character; his education and the circumstances which surrounded him have made him a criminal, and for these he is not responsible. All these opinions are extremely plausible; and so long as the question is argued as one of justice simply, without going down to the principles which lie under justice and are the source of its authority, I am unable to see how any of these reasoners can be refuted. For in truth every one of the three builds upon rules of justice confessedly true. The first appeals to the acknowledged injustice of singling out an individual and making him a sacrifice, without his consent, for other people's benefit. The second relies on the acknowledged justice of self-defense and the admitted injustice of forcing one person to conform to another's notions of what constitutes his good. The Owenite invokes the admitted principle that it is unjust to punish anyone for what he cannot help. Each is triumphant so long as he is not compelled to take into consideration any other maxims of justice than the one he has selected; but as soon as their several maxims are brought face to face, each disputant seems to have exactly as much to say for himself as the others. No one of them can carry out his own notion of justice without trampling upon another equally binding. These are difficulties; they have always been felt to be such; and many devices have been invented to turn rather than to overcome them. As a refuge from the last of the three, men imagined what they called the freedom of the will—fancying that they could not justify punishing a man whose will is in a thoroughly hateful state unless it be supposed to have come into that state through no influence of anterior circumstances. To escape from the other difficulties, a favorite contrivance has been the fiction of a contract whereby at some unknown period all the members of society engaged to obey the laws and consented to be punished for any disobedience to them, thereby giving to their legislators the right, which it is assumed they would not otherwise have had, of punishing them, either for their own good or for that of society. This happy thought was considered to get rid of the whole difficulty and to legitimate the infliction of punishment, in virtue of another received maxim of justice, *volenti non fit injuria*—that is not unjust which is done with the consent of the person who is supposed to be hurt by it. I need hardly remark that, even if the consent were not a mere fiction, this maxim is not superior in authority to the others which it is brought in to supersede. It is, on the contrary, an instructive specimen of the loose and irregular manner in which supposed principles of justice grow up. This particular one evidently came into use as a help to the coarse exigencies of court of law, which are sometimes obliged to be content with very uncertain presumptions, on account of the greater evils which would often arise from any attempt on their part to cut finer. But even courts of law are not able to adhere consistently to the maxim, for they allow voluntary engagements to be set aside on the ground of fraud, and sometimes on that of mere mistake or misinformation.

Again, when the legitimacy of inflicting punishment is admitted, how many conflicting conceptions of justice come to light in discussing the proper apportionment of punishments to offenses. No rule on the subject recommends itself so strongly to the primitive and spontaneous sentiment of justice as the *lex talionis,* an eye for an eye and a tooth for a tooth. Though this principle of the Jewish and of the Mohammedan law has been generally abandoned in Europe as a practical maxim, there is, I suspect, in most minds, a secret hankering after it; and when retribution accidentally falls on an offender in that precise shape, the general feeling of satisfaction evinced bears witness how natural is the sentiment to which this repayment in kind is acceptable. With many, the test of justice in penal infliction is that the punishment should be proportioned to the offense, meaning that it should be exactly measured by the moral guilt of the culprit (whatever be their standard for measuring moral guilt), the consideration what amount of punishment is necessary to deter from the offense having nothing to do with the question of justice, in their estimation; while there are others to whom that consideration is all in all, who maintain that it is not just, at least for man, to inflict on a fellow creature, whatever may be his offenses, any amount of suffering beyond the least that will suffice to prevent him from repeating, and others from imitating, his misconduct.

To take another example from a subject already once referred to. In co-operative industrial association, is it just or not that talent or skill should give a title to superior remuneration? On the negative side of the question it is argued that whoever does the best he can deserves equally well, and ought not in justice to be put in a position of inferiority for no fault of his own; that superior abilities have already advantages more than enough, in the admiration they excite, the personal influence they command, and the internal sources of satisfaction attending them, without adding to these a superior share of the world's goods; and that society is bound in justice rather to make compensation to the less favored for this unmerited inequality of advantages than to aggravate it. On the contrary side it is contended that society receives more from the more efficient laborer; that, his services being more useful, society owes him a larger return for them; that a greater share of the joint result is actually his work, and not to allow his claim to it is a kind of robbery; that, if he is only to receive as much as others, he can only be justly required to produce as much, and to give a smaller amount of time and exertion, proportioned to his superior efficiency. Who shall decide between these appeals to conflicting principles of justice? Justice has in this case two sides to it, which it is impossible to bring into harmony, and the two disputants have chosen opposite sides; the one looks to what it is just that the individual should receive, the other to what it is just that the community should give. Each, from his own point of view, is unanswerable; and any choice between them, on grounds of justice, must be perfectly arbitrary. Social utility alone can decide the preference.

How many, again, and how irreconcilable are the standards of justice to which reference is made in discussing the repartition of taxation. One opinion is that payment to the state should be in numerical proportion to pecuniary means. Others think that justice dictates what they term graduated taxation—taking a higher percentage from those who have more to spare. In point of natural justice a strong case might be made for disregarding means altogether, and taking the same absolute sum (whenever it could be got) from everyone; as the subscribers to a mess or to a club all pay the same sum for the same privileges, whether they can all equally afford it or not. Since the protection (it might be said) of law and government is afforded to and is equally required by all, there is no injustice in making all buy it at the same price. It is reckoned justice, not injustice, that a dealer should charge to all customers the same price for the same article, not a price varying according to their means of payment. This doctrine, as applied to taxation, finds no advocates because it conflicts so strongly with man's feelings of humanity and of social expediency; but the principle of justice which it invokes is as true and as binding as those which can be appealed to against it. Accordingly it exerts a tacit influence on the line of defense employed for other modes of assessing taxation. People feel obliged to argue that the state does more for the rich man than for the poor, as a justification for its taking more from them, though this is in reality not true, for the rich would be far better able to protect themselves, in the absence of law or government, than the poor, and indeed would probably be successful in converting the poor into their slaves. Others, again, so far defer to the same conception of justice as to maintain that all should pay an equal capitation tax for the protection of their persons (these being of equal value to all), and an unequal tax for the protection of their property, which is unequal. To this others reply that the all of one man is as valuable to him as the all of another. From these confusions there is no other mode of extrication than the utilitarian.

Is, then, the difference between the just and the expedient a merely imaginary distinction? Have mankind been under a delusion in thinking that justice is a more sacred thing than policy, and that the latter ought only to be listened to after the former has been satisfied? By no means. The exposition we have given of the nature and origin of the sentiment recognizes a real distinction; and no one of those who profess the most sublime contempt for the consequences of actions as an element in their morality attaches more importance to the distinction than I do. While I dispute the pretensions of any theory which sets up an imaginary standard of justice not grounded on utility, I account the justice which is grounded on utility to be the chief part, and incomparably the most sacred and binding part, of all morality. Justice is a name for certain classes of moral rules which concern the essentials of human well-being more nearly, and are therefore of more absolute obligation, than any other rules for the guidance of life; and the notion which we have found to be of the essence of the idea of justice—that of a right residing in an individual—implies and testifies to this more binding obligation.

The moral rules which forbid mankind to hurt one another (in which we must never forget to include wrongful interference with each other's freedom) are more vital to human well-being than any maxims, however important, which only point out the best mode of managing some department of human affairs. They have also the peculiarity that they are the main element in determining the whole of the social feelings of mankind. It is their observance which alone preserves peace among human beings; if obedience to them were not the rule, and disobedience the exception, everyone would see in everyone else an enemy against whom he must be perpetually guarding himself. What is hardly less important, these are the precepts which mankind have the strongest and the most direct inducements for impressing upon one another. By merely giving to each other prudential instruction or exhortation, they may gain, or think they gain, nothing; in inculcating on each other the duty of positive beneficence, they have an unmistakable interest, but far less in degree; a person may possibly not need the benefits of others, but he always needs that they should not do him hurt. Thus the moralities which protect every individual from being harmed by others, either directly or by being hindered in his freedom of pursuing his own good, are at once those which he himself has most at heart and those which he has the strongest interest in publishing and enforcing by word and deed. It is by a person's observance of these that his fitness to exist as one of the fellowship of human beings is tested and decided; for on that depends his being a nuisance or not to those with whom he is in contact. Now it is these moralities primarily which compose the obligations of justice. The most marked cases of injustice, and those which give the tone to the feeling of repugnance which characterizes the sentiment, are acts of wrongful aggression or wrongful exercise of power over someone; the next are those which consist in wrongfully withholding from him something which is his due—in both cases inflicting on him a positive hurt, either in the form of direct suffering or of the privation of some good which he had reasonable ground, either of a physical or of a social kind, for counting upon.

The same powerful motives which command the observance of these primary moralities enjoin the punishment of those who violate them; and as the impulses of self-defense, of defense of others, and of vengeance are all called forth against such persons, retribution, or evil for evil, becomes closely connected with the sentiment of justice, and is universally included in the idea. Good for good is also one of the dictates of justice; and this, though its social utility is evident, and though it carries with it a natural human feeling, has not at first sight that obvious connection with hurt or injury which, existing in the most elementary cases of just and unjust, is the source of the characteristic intensity of the sentiment. But the connection, though less obvious, is not less real. He who accepts benefits and denies a return of them when needed inflicts a real hurt by disappointing one of the most natural and reasonable of expectations, and one which he must at least tacitly have encouraged, otherwise the benefits would seldom have been conferred. The important rank, among human evils and wrongs, of the disappointment of expectation is shown in the fact that it constitutes the principal criminality of two such highly immoral acts as a breach of friendship and a breach of promise. Few hurts which human beings can sustain are greater, and none wound more, than when that on which they habitually and with full assurance relied fails them in the hour of need; and few wrongs are greater than this mere withholding of good; none excite more resentment, either in the person suffering or in a sympathizing spectator. The principle, therefore, of giving to each what they deserve, that is, good for good as well as evil for evil, is not only included within the idea of justice as we have defined it, but is a proper object of that intensity of sentiment which places the just in human estimation above the simply expedient.

Most of the maxims of justice current in the world, and commonly appealed to in its transactions, are simply instrumental to carrying into effect the principles of justice which we have now spoken of. That a person is only responsible for what he has done voluntarily, or could voluntarily have avoided, that it is unjust to condemn any person unheard; that the punishment ought to be proportioned to the offense, and the like, are maxims intended to prevent the just principle of evil for evil from being perverted to the infliction of evil without that justification. The greater part of these common maxims have come into use from the practice of courts of justice, which have been naturally led to a more complete recognition and elaboration than was likely to suggest itself to others, of the rules necessary to enable them to fulfill their double function—of inflicting punishment when due, and of awarding to each person his right.

That first of judicial virtues, impartiality, is an obligation of justice, partly for the reason last mentioned, as being a necessary condition of the fulfillment of other obligations of justice. But this is not the only source of the exalted rank, among human obligations, of those maxims of equality and impartiality, which, both in popular estimation and in that of the most enlightened, are included among the precepts of justice. In one point of view, they may be considered as corollaries from the principles already laid down. If it is a duty to do to each according to his deserts, returning good for good, as well as repressing evil by evil, it necessarily follows that we should treat all equally well (when no higher duty forbids) who have deserved equally well of *us,* and that society should treat all equally well who have deserved equally well of *it,* that is, who have deserved equally well absolutely. This is the highest abstract standard of social and distributive justice, toward which all institutions and the efforts of all virtuous citizens should be made in the utmost possible degree to converge. But this great moral duty rests upon a still deeper foundation, being a direct emanation from the first principle of morals, and not a mere logical corollary from secondary or derivative doctrines. It is involved in the very meaning of utility, or the greatest happiness principle. That principle is a mere form of words without rational signification unless one person's happiness, supposed equal in degree (with the proper allowance made for kind), is counted for exactly as much as another's. Those conditions being supplied, Bentham's dictum, "everybody to count for one, nobody for more than one," might be written under the principle of utility as an explanatory commentary.[2] The equal claim of everybody to happiness, in the estimation

[2] This implication, in the first principle of the utilitarian scheme, of perfect impartiality between persons is regarded by Mr. Herbert Spencer (in his *Social Statics*) as a disproof of the pretensions of utility to be a sufficient guide to right; since (he says) the principle of utility presupposes the anterior principle that everybody has an equal right to happiness. It may be more correctly described as supposing that equal amounts of happiness are equally desirable, whether felt by the same or different persons. This, however, is not a *pre*-suppostion, not a premise needful to support the principle of utility, but the very principle itself; for what is the principle of utility if it be not that "happiness" and "desirable" are synonymous terms? If there is any anterior principle implied, it can be no other than this, that the truths of arithmetic are applicable to the valuation of happiness, as of all other measurable quantities.

(Mr. Herbert Spencer, in a private communication on the subject of the preceding note, objects to being considered an opponent of utilitarianism and states that he regards happiness as the ultimate end of morality; but deems that end only partially attainable by empirical generalizations from the observed results of conduct, and completely attainable only by deducing, from the laws of life and the conditions of existence, what kinds of action necessarily tend to produce happiness, and what kinds to produce unhappiness. With the excep-

of the moralist and of the legislator, involves an equal claim to all the means of happiness except in so far as the inevitable conditions of human life and the general interest in which that of every individual is included set limits to the maxim; and those limits ought to be strictly construed. As every other maxim of justice, so this is by no means applied or held applicable universally; on the contrary, as I have already remarked, it bends to every person's ideas of social expediency. But in whatever case it is deemed applicable at all, it is held to be the dictate of justice. All persons are deemed to have a *right* to equality of treatment, except when some recognized social expediency requires the reverse. And hence all social inequalities which have ceased to be considered expedient assume the character, not of simple inexpediency, but of injustice, and appear so tyrannical that people are apt to wonder how they ever could have been tolerated—forgetful that they themselves, perhaps, tolerate other inequalities under an equally mistaken notion of expediency, the correction of which would make that which they approve seem quite as monstrous as what they have at last learned to condemn. The entire history of social improvement has been a series of transitions by which one custom or institution after another, from being a supposed primary necessity of social existence, has passed into the rank of a universally stigmatized injustice and tyranny. So it has been with the distinctions of slaves and freemen, nobles and serfs, patricians and plebeians; and so it will be, and in part already is, with the aristocracies of color, race, and sex.

It appears from what has been said that justice is a name for certain moral requirements which, regarded collectively, stand higher in the scale of social utility, and are therefore of more paramount

---

tion of the word "necessarily," I have no dissent to express from this doctrine; and (omitting that word) I am not aware that any modern advocate of utilitarianism is of a different opinion. Bentham, certainly, to whom in the *Social Statics* Mr. Spencer particularly referred, is, least of all writers, chargeable with unwillingness to deduce the effect of actions on happiness from the laws of human nature and the universal conditions of human life. The common charge against him is of relying too exclusively upon such deductions and declining altogether to be bound by the generalizations from specific experience which Mr. Spencer thinks that utilitarians generally confine themselves to. My own opinion (and, as I collect, Mr. Spencer's) is that in ethics, as in all other branches of scientific study, the consilience of the results of both these processes, each corroborating and verifying the other, is requisite to give to any general proposition the kind and degree of evidence which constitutes scientific proof.)

obligation, than any others, though particular cases may occur in which some other social duty is so important as to overrule any one of the general maxims of justice. Thus, to save a life, it may not only be allowable, but a duty, to steal or take by force the necessary food or medicine, or to kidnap and compel to officiate the only qualified medical practitioner. In such cases, as we do not call anything justice which is not a virtue, we usually say, not that justice must give way to some other moral principle, but that what is just in ordinary cases is, by reason of the other principle, not just in the particular case. By this useful accommodation of language, the character of indefeasibility attributed to justice is kept up, and we are saved from the necessity of maintaining that there can be laudable injustice.

The considerations which have now been adduced resolve, I conceive, the only real difficulty in the utilitarian theory of morals. It has always been evident that all cases of justice are also cases of expediency; the difference is in the peculiar sentiment which attaches to the former, as contradistinguished from the latter. If this characteristic sentiment has been sufficiently accounted for; if there is no necessity to assume for it any peculiarity of origin; if it is simply the natural feeling of resentment, moralized by being made coextensive with the demands of social good; and if this feeling not only does but ought to exist in all the classes of cases to which the idea of justice corresponds—that idea no longer presents itself as a stumbling block to the utilitarian ethics. Justice remains the appropriate name for certain social utilities which are vastly more important, and therefore more absolute and imperative, than any others are as a class (though not more so than others may be in particular cases); and which, therefore, ought to be, as well as naturally are, guarded by a sentiment, not only different in degree, but also in kind; distinguished from the milder feeling which attaches to the mere idea of promoting human pleasure or convenience at once by the more definite nature of its commands and by the sterner character of its sanctions.

DAVID HUME

Justice and Equality

1

. . . I have already observed that justice takes its rise from human conventions; and that these are intended as a remedy to some inconveniences, which proceed from the concurrence of certain *qualities* of the human mind with the *situation* of external objects. The qualities of the mind are *selfishness* and *limited generosity.* And the situation of external objects is their *easy change,* joined to their *scarcity* in comparison of the wants and desires of men. But however philosophers may have been bewildered in those speculations, poets have been guided more infallibly, by a certain taste or common instinct, which in most kinds of reasoning goes farther than any of that art and philosophy, with which we have been yet acquainted. They easily perceived, if every man had a tender regard for another, or if nature supplied abundantly all our wants and desires, that the jealousy of interest, which justice supposes, could no longer have place; nor would there be any occasion for those distinctions and limits of property and possession, which at present are in use among mankind. Increase to a sufficient degree the benevolence of men, or the bounty of nature, and you render justice useless, by supplying its place with much nobler virtues, and more valuable blessings. The selfishness of men is animated by the few

From *A Treatise of Human Nature* (1739), Book III, Part II, Sec. II (with omissions), and *An Enquiry Concerning the Principles of Morals* (1751), Sec. III, Part II (with omissions). Spelling and punctuation have been revised in accordance with current usage. Italics are as in the original.

possessions we have, in proportion to our wants; and it is to restrain this selfishness, that men have been obliged to separate themselves from the community, and to distinguish between their own goods and those of others.

Nor need we have recourse to the fictions of poets to learn this; but beside the reason of the thing, may discover the same truth by common experience and observation. It is easy to remark, that a cordial affection renders all things common among friends; and that married people in particular mutually lose their property, and are unacquainted with the *mine* and *thine,* which are so necessary, and yet cause such disturbance in human society. The same effect arises from any alteration in the circumstances of mankind; as when there is such a plenty of anything as satisfies all the desires of men. In which case the distinction of property is entirely lost, and everything remains in common. This we may observe with regard to air and water, though the most valuable of all external objects; and may easily conclude, that if men were supplied with everything in the same abundance, or if *everyone* had the same affection and tender regard for *everyone* as for himself, justice and injustice would be equally unknown among mankind.

Here then is a proposition, which, I think, may be regarded as certain, *that it is only from the selfishness and confined generosity of men, along with the scanty provision nature has made for his wants, that justice derives its origin.* If we look backward we shall find that this proposition bestows an additional force on some of those observations which we have already made on this subject.

First, we may conclude from it, that a regard to public interest, or a strong extensive benevolence, is not our first and original motive for the observation of the rules of justice; since it is allowed, that if men were endowed with such a benevolence, these rules would never have been dreamed of.

Secondly, we may conclude from the same principle, that the sense of justice is not founded on reason, or on the discovery of certain connexions and relations of ideas, which are eternal, immutable, and universally obligatory. For since it is confessed, that such an alteration as that above-mentioned, in the temper and circumstances of mankind, would entirely alter our duties and obligations, it is necessary upon the common system, *that the sense of virtue is derived from reason,* to show the change which this must produce in the relations and ideas. But it is evident, that the only cause, why the extensive generosity of man, and the perfect abundance of everything, would destroy the very idea of justice, is because they render it useless; and that, on the other hand, his confined benevolence, and his necessitous condition, give rise to that virtue, only by making it requisite to the public interest, and to that of every individual. It was therefore a concern for our own, and the public interest, which made us establish the laws of justice; and nothing can be more certain, than that it is not any relation of ideas, which gives us this concern, but our impressions and sentiments, without which everything in nature is perfectly indifferent to us, and can never in the least affect us. The sense of justice, therefore, is not founded on our ideas, but on our impressions.

Thirdly, we may farther confirm the foregoing proposition, *that those impressions, which give rise to this sense of justice, are not natural to the mind of man, but arise from artifice and human conventions.* For since any considerable alteration of temper and circumstances destroys equally justice and injustice; and since such an alteration has an effect only by changing our own and the public interest; it follows, that the first establishment of the rules of justice depends on these different interests. But if men pursued the public interest naturally, and with a hearty affection, they would never have dreamed of restraining each other by these rules; and if they pursued their own interest, without any precaution, they would run head-long into every kind of injustice and violence. These rules, therefore, are artificial, and seek their end in an oblique and indirect manner; nor is the interest, which gives rise to them, of a kind that could be pursued by the natural and inartificial passions of men.

To make this more evident, consider, that though the rules of justice are established merely by interest, their connexion with interest is somewhat singular, and is different from what may be observed on other occasions. A single act of justice is frequently contrary to *public interest;* and were it to stand alone, without being followed by other acts, may, in itself, be very prejudicial to society. When a man of merit, of a beneficent disposition, restores a great fortune to a miser, or a seditious bigot, he has acted justly and laudably, but the public is a real sufferer. Nor is every single act of justice, considered apart, more conducive to private interest, than to public; and it is easily conceived how a man may impoverish himself by a single instance of integrity, and have reason to wish that with regard to that single act, the laws of justice were for a moment suspended in the universe. But however single acts of justice may be contrary, either to public or private interest, it is certain, that the whole plan or scheme is highly conducive, or indeed absolutely requisite, both to the support of society, and the well-being of every individual. It is impossible to separate the good from the ill. Property must be stable, and must be fixed by general rules. Though in one instance the public be a sufferer, this momentary ill is amply compensated by the steady prosecution of the rule, and by the peace and order, which it establishes in society. And even every individual person must find himself a gainer, on balancing the account; since, without justice, society must immediately dissolve, and everyone must fall into that savage and solitary condition, which is infinitely worse than the worst situation that can possibly be supposed in society. When therefore men have had experience enough to observe that whatever may be the consequence of any single act of justice performed by a single person, yet the whole system of actions, concurred in by the whole society, is infinitely advantageous to the whole, and to every part; it is not long before justice and property take place. Every member of society is sensible of this interest. Everyone expresses this sense to his fellows, along with the resolution he has taken of squaring his actions by it, on condition that others will do the same. No more is requisite to induce any one of them to perform an act of justice, who has the first opportunity. This becomes an example to others. And thus justice establishes itself by a kind of convention or agreement; that is, by a sense of interest, supposed to be common to all and where every single act is performed in expectation that others are to perform the like. Without such a convention no one would ever have dreamed that there was such a virtue as justice, or have been induced to conform his actions to it. Taking any single act, my justice may be pernicious in every respect; and it is only upon the supposition, that others are to imitate my example, that I can be induced to embrace that virtue; since nothing but this combination can render justice advantageous, or afford me any motives to conform myself to its rules.

• • • • • • • • • • • •

2

If we examine the *particular* laws by which justice is directed and property determined we shall still be presented with the same conclusion. The good of mankind is the only object of all these laws and regulations. Not only it is requisite for the peace and interest of society that men's possessions should be separated but the rules, which we follow in making the separation are such as can best be contrived to serve farther the interests of society.

We shall suppose that a creature possessed of reason but unacquainted with human nature, deliberates with himself what rules of justice or property would best promote public interest, and establish peace and security among mankind. His most obvious thought would be, to assign the largest possessions to the most extensive virtue, and give everyone the power of doing good, proportioned to his inclination. In a perfect theocracy where a being infinitely intelligent governs by particular volitions, this rule would certainly have place and might serve to the wisest purposes. But were mankind to execute such a law, so great is the uncertainty of merit, both from its natural obscurity, and from the self-conceit of each individual, that no determinate rule of conduct would ever result from it; and the total dissolution of society must be the immediate consequence. Fanatics may suppose *that dominion is founded on grace,* and *that saints alone inherit the earth,* but the civil magistrate very justly puts these sublime theorists on the same footing with common robbers, and teaches them by the severest discipline that a rule which, in speculation, may seem the most advantageous to society, may yet be found in practice totally pernicious and destructive.

That there were *religious* fanatics of this kind in England, during the civil wars, we learn from history; though it is probable, that the obvious *tendency* of these principles excited such horror in mankind, as soon obliged the dangerous enthusiasts to renounce, or at least conceal their tenets. Perhaps the *levellers,* who claimed an equal distribution of property, were a kind of *political* fanatics which arose from the religious species and more openly avowed their pretensions; as carrying a more plausible appearance, of being practicable in themselves as well as useful to human society.

It must, indeed, be confessed that nature is so liberal to mankind that, were all her presents equally divided among the species, and improved by art and industry, every individual would enjoy all the necessaries, and even most of the comforts of life, nor would ever be liable to any ills, but such as might accidentally arise from the sickly frame and constitution of his body. It must also be confessed that wherever we depart from this equality, we rob the poor of more satisfaction than we add to the rich, and that the slight gratification of a frivolous vanity in one individual frequently costs more than bread to many families, and even provinces. It may appear withal, that the rule of equality, as it would be highly *useful,* is not altogether *impracticable,* but has taken place, at least in an imperfect degree, in some republics, particularly that of Sparta, where it was attended, it is said, with the most beneficial consequences. Not to mention that the Agrarian laws, so frequently claimed in Rome, and carried into execution in many Greek cities, proceeded all of them from a general idea of the utility of this principle.

But historians and even common sense may inform us, that, however specious these ideas of *perfect* equality may seem, they are really, at bottom, *impracticable;* and were they not so, would be extremely *pernicious* to human society. Render possessions ever so equal, men's different degrees of art, care, and industry will immediately break that equality. Or if you check these virtues, you reduce society to the most extreme indigence; and instead of preventing want and beggary in a few, render it unavoidable to the whole community. The most rigorous inquisition too is requisite to watch every inequality on its first appearance; and the most severe jurisdiction to punish and redress it. But besides that so much authority must soon degenerate into tyranny and be exerted with great partialities; who can possibly be possessed of it in such a situation as is here supposed? Perfect equality of possessions destroying all subordination weakens extremely the authority of magistracy and must reduce all power nearly to a level, as well as property.

We may conclude, therefore, that in order to establish laws for the regulation of property we must be acquainted with the nature and situation of man; must reject appearances, which may be false, though specious; and must search for those rules, which are, on the whole, most *useful* and *beneficial.* Vulgar sense and slight experience are sufficient for this purpose; where men give not way to too selfish avidity or too extensive enthusiasm. . . .

JOHN RAWLS

Justice as Fairness

1

It might seem at first sight that the concepts of justice and fairness are the same, and that there is no reason to distinguish them, or to say that one is more fundamental than the other. I think that this impression is mistaken. In this paper I wish to show that the fundamental idea in the concept of justice is fairness; and I wish to offer an analysis of the concept of justice from this point of view. To bring out the force of this claim, and the analysis based upon it, I shall then argue that it is this aspect of justice for which utilitarianism, in its classical form, is unable to account, but which is expressed, even if misleadingly, by the idea of the social contract.

To start with I shall develop a particular conception of justice by stating and commenting upon two principles which specify it, and by considering the circumstances and conditions under which they may be thought to arise. The principles defining this conception, and the conception itself, are, of course, familiar. It may be possible, however, by using the notion of fairness as a framework, to assemble and to look at them in a new way. Before stating this conception, however, the following preliminary matters should be kept in mind.

John Rawls, "Justice as Fairness," *The Philosophical Review,* LXVII (April 1958), pp. 164–94. Reprinted by permission. Some footnotes have been omitted, others abbreviated, and the last paragraph of section 3 has been revised by the author.

Throughout I consider justice only as a virtue of social institutions, or what I shall call practices.[1] The principles of justice are regarded as formulating restrictions as to how practices may define positions and offices, and assign thereto powers and liabilities, rights and duties. Justice as a virtue of particular actions or of persons I do not take up at all. It is important to distinguish these various subjects of justice, since the meaning of the concept varies according to whether it is applied to practices, particular actions, or persons. These meanings are, indeed, connected, but they are not identical. I shall confine my discussion to the sense of justice as applied to practices, since this sense is the basic one. Once it is understood, the other senses should go quite easily.

Justice is to be understood in its customary sense as representing but *one* of the many virtues of social institutions, for these may be antiquated, inefficient, degrading, or any number of other things, without being unjust. Justice is not to be confused with an all-inclusive vision of a good society; it is only one part of any such conception. It is important, for example, to distinguish that sense of equality which is an aspect of the concept of justice from that sense of equality which belongs to a more comprehensive social ideal. There may well be inequalities which one concedes are just, or at least not unjust, but which, nevertheless, one wishes, on other grounds, to do away with. I shall focus attention, then, on the usual sense of justice in which it is essentially the elimination of arbitrary distinctions and the establishment, within the structure of a practice, of a proper balance between competing claims.

Finally, there is no need to consider the principles discussed below as *the* principles of justice. For the moment it is sufficient that they are typical of a family of principles normally associated with the concept of justice. The way in which the principles of this family resemble one another, as shown by the background against which they may be thought to arise, will be made clear by the whole of the subsequent argument.

[1] I use the word "practice" throughout as a sort of technical term meaning any form of activity specified by a system of rules which defines offices, roles, moves, penalties, defences, and so on, and which gives the activity its structure. As examples one may think of games and rituals, trials and parliaments, markets and systems of property. I have attempted a partial analysis of the notion of a practice in a paper, "Two Concepts of Rules," *Philosophical Review*, LXIV (1955), pp. 3–32.

2

The conception of justice which I want to develop may be stated in the form of two principles as follows: first, each person participating in a practice, or affected by it, has an equal right to the most extensive liberty compatible with a like liberty for all; and second, inequalities are arbitrary unless it is reasonable to expect that they will work out for everyone's advantage, and provided the positions and offices to which they attach, or from which they may be gained, are open to all. These principles express justice as a complex of three ideas: liberty, equality, and reward for services contributing to the common good.[2]

The term "person" is to be construed variously depending on the circumstances. On some occasions it will mean human individuals, but in others it may refer to nations, provinces, business firms, churches, teams, and so on. The principles of justice apply in all these instances, although there is a certain logical priority to the case of human individuals. As I shall use the term "person," it will be ambiguous in the manner indicated.

The first principle holds, of course, only if other things are equal: that is, while there must always be a justification for departing from the initial position of equal liberty (which is defined by the pattern of rights and duties, powers and liabilities, established by a practice), and the burden of proof is placed on him who would depart from it, nevertheless, there can be, and often there is, a justification for doing so. Now, that similar particular cases, as defined by a practice, should be treated similarly as they arise, is part of the very concept of a practice; it is involved in the notion

[2] These principles are, of course, well known in one form or another and appear in many analyses of justice even where the writers differ widely on other matters. Thus if the principle of equal liberty is commonly associated with Kant (see *The Philosophy of Law,* tr. W. Hastie, Edinburgh, 1887, pp. 56 f.), it may be claimed that it can also be found in J. S. Mill's *On Liberty* and elsewhere, and in many other liberal writers. Recently H. L. A. Hart has argued for something like it in his paper, "Are There Any Natural Rights?" *Philosophical Review,* LXIV (1955), pp. 175–91. The injustice of inequalities which are not won in return for a contribution to the common advantage is, of course, widespread in political writings of all sorts. The conception of justice here discussed is distinctive, if at all, only in selecting these two principles in this form; but for another similar analysis, see the discussion by W. D. Lamont, *The Principles of Moral Judgment* (Oxford, 1946), Chap. v.

of an activity in accordance with rules. The first principle expresses an analogous conception, but as applied to the structure of practices themselves. It holds, for example, that there is a presumption against the distinctions and classifications made by legal systems and other practices to the extent that they infringe on the original and equal liberty of the persons participating in them. The second principle defines how this presumption may be rebutted.

It might be argued at this point that justice requires only an equal liberty. If, however, a greater liberty were possible for all without loss or conflict, then it would be irrational to settle on a lesser liberty. There is no reason for circumscribing rights unless their exercise would be incompatible, or would render the practice defining them less effective. Therefore no serious distortion of the concept of justice is likely to follow from including within it the concept of the greatest equal liberty.

The second principle defines what sorts of inequalities are permissible; it specifies how the presumption laid down by the first principle may be put aside. Now by inequalities it is best to understand not *any* differences between offices and positions, but differences in the benefits and burdens attached to them either directly or indirectly, such as prestige and wealth, or liability to taxation and compulsory services. Players in a game do not protest against there being different positions, such as batter, pitcher, catcher, and the like, nor to there being various privileges and powers as specified by the rules; nor do the citizens of a country object to there being the different offices of government such as president, senator, governor, judge, and so on, each with their special rights and duties. It is not differences of this kind that are normally thought of as inequalities, but differences in the resulting distribution established by a practice, or made possible by it, of the things men strive to attain or avoid. Thus they may complain about the pattern of honors and rewards set up by a practice (*e.g.* the privileges and salaries of government officials) or they may object to the distribution of power and wealth which results from the various ways in which men avail themselves of the opportunities allowed by it (*e.g.* the concentration of wealth which may develop in a free price system allowing large entrepreneurial or speculative gains).

It should be noted that the second principle holds that an inequality is allowed only if there is reason to believe that the practice with the inequality, or resulting in it, will work for the advantage of *every* party engaging in it. Here it is important to stress that *every* party must gain from the inequality. Since the principle applies to practices, it implies that the representative man in every office or position defined by a practice, when he views it as a going concern, must find it reasonable to prefer his condition and prospects with the inequality to what they would be under the practice without it. The principle excludes, therefore, the justification of inequalities on the grounds that the disadvantages of those in one position are outweighed by the greater advantages of those in another position. This rather simple restriction is the main modification I wish to make in the utilitarian principle as usually understood. When coupled with the notion of a practice, it is a restriction of consequence, and one which some utilitarians, for example Hume and Mill, have used in their discussions of justice without realizing apparently its significance, or at least without calling attention to it. Why it is a significant modification of principle, changing one's conception of justice entirely, the whole of my argument will show.

Further, it is also necessary that the various offices to which special benefits or burdens attach are open to all. It may be, for example, to the common advantage, as just defined, to attach special benefits to certain offices. Perhaps by doing so the requisite talent can be attracted to them and encouraged to give its best efforts. But any offices having special benefits must be won in a fair competition in which contestants are judged on their merits. If some offices were not open, those excluded would normally be justified in feeling unjustly treated, even if they benefited from the greater efforts of those who were allowed to compete for them. Now if one can assume that offices are open, it is necessary only to consider the design of practices themselves and how they jointly, as a system, work together. It will be a mistake to focus attention on the varying relative positions of particular persons, who may be known to us by their proper names, and to require that each such change, as a once for all transaction viewed in isolation, must be in itself just. It is the system of practices which is to be judged, and judged from a general point of view: unless one is prepared to criticize it from the standpoint of a representative man holding some particular office, one has no complaint against it.

3

Given these principles one might try to derive them from *a priori* principles of reason, or claim that they were known by intuition. These are familiar enough steps and, at least in the case of the first principle, might be made with some success. Usually, however, such arguments, made at this point, are unconvincing. They are not likely to lead to an understanding of the basis of the principles of justice, not at least as principles of justice. I wish, therefore, to look at the principles in a different way.

Imagine a society of persons amongst whom a certain system of practices is *already* well established. Now suppose that by and large they are mutually self-interested; their allegiance to their established practices is normally founded on the prospect of self-advantage. One need not assume that, in all senses of the term "person," the persons in this society are mutually self-interested. If the characterization as mutually self-interested applies when the line of division is the family, it may still be true that members of families are bound by ties of sentiment and affection and willingly acknowledge duties in contradiction to self-interest. Mutual self-interestedness in the relations between families, nations, churches, and the like, is commonly associated with intense loyalty and devotion on the part of individual members. Therefore, one can form a more realistic conception of this society if one thinks of it as consisting of mutually self-interested families, or some other association. Further, it is not necessary to suppose that these persons are mutually self-interested under all circumstances, but only in the usual situations in which they participate in their common practices.

Now suppose also that these persons are rational: they know their own interests more or less accurately; they are capable of tracing out the likely consequences of adopting one practice rather than another; they are capable of adhering to a course of action once they have decided upon it; they can resist present temptations and the enticements of immediate gain; and the bare knowledge or perception of the difference between their condition and that of others is not, within certain limits and in itself, a source of great dissatisfaction. Only the last point adds anything to the usual definition of rationality. This definition should allow, I think, for the idea that a rational man would not be greatly downcast from knowing, or seeing, that others are in a better position than himself, unless he thought their being so was the result of injustice, or the consequence of letting chance work itself out for no useful common purpose, and so on. So if these persons strike us as unpleasantly egoistic, they are at least free in some degree from the fault of envy.[3]

Finally, assume that these persons have roughly similar needs and interests, or needs and interests in various ways complementary, so that fruitful cooperation amongst them is possible; and suppose that they are sufficiently equal in power and ability to guarantee that in normal circumstances none is able to dominate the others. This condition (as well as the others) may seem excessively vague; but in view of the conception of justice to which the argument leads, there seems no reason for making it more exact here.

Since these persons are conceived as engaging in their common practices, which are already established, there is no question of our supposing them to come together to deliberate as to how they will set these practices up for the first time. Yet we can imagine that from time to time they discuss with one another whether any of them has a legitimate complaint against their established institutions. Such discussions are perfectly natural in any normal society. Now suppose that they have settled on doing this in the following way. They first try to arrive at the principles by which complaints, and so practices themselves, are to be judged. Their procedure for this is to let each person propose the principles upon which he wishes his complaints to be tried with the understanding that, if acknowledged, the complaints of others will be similarly tried, and that no complaints will be heard at all until everyone is roughly of one mind as to how complaints are to be judged. They each understand further that the principles proposed and acknowledged on this occasion are binding on future occasions. Thus each will be wary of proposing a principle which would

[3] It is not possible to discuss here this addition to the usual conception of rationality. If it seems peculiar, it may be worth remarking that it is analogous to the modification of the utilitarian principle which the argument as a whole is designed to explain and justify. In the same way that the satisfaction of interests, the representative claims of which violate the principles of justice, is not a reason for having a practice (see sec. 7), unfounded envy, within limits, need not to be taken into account.

give him a peculiar advantage, in his present circumstances, supposing it to be accepted. Each person knows that he will be bound by it in future circumstances the peculiarities of which cannot be known, and which might well be such that the principle is then to his disadvantage. The idea is that everyone should be required to make *in advance* a firm commitment, which others also may reasonably be expected to make, and that no one be given the opportunity to tailor the canons of a legitimate complaint to fit his own special condition, and then to discard them when they no longer suit his purpose. Hence each person will propose principles of a general kind which will, to a large degree, gain their sense from the various applications to be made of them, the particular circumstances of which being as yet unknown. These principles will express the conditions in accordance with which each is the least unwilling to have his interests limited in the design of practices, given the competing interests of the others, on the supposition that the interests of others will be limited likewise. The restrictions which would so arise might be thought of as those a person would keep in mind if he were designing a practice in which his enemy were to assign him his place.

The two main parts of this conjectural account have a definite significance. The character and respective situations of the parties reflect the typical circumstances in which questions of justice arise. The procedure whereby principles are proposed and acknowledged represents constraints, analogous to those of having a morality, whereby rational and mutually self-interested persons are brought to act reasonably. Thus the first part reflects the fact that questions of justice arise when conflicting claims are made upon the design of a practice and where it is taken for granted that each person will insist, as far as possible, on what he considers his rights. It is typical of cases of justice to involve persons who are pressing on one another their claims, between which a fair balance or equilibrium must be found. On the other hand, as expressed by the second part, having a morality must at least imply the acknowledgement of principles as impartially applying to one's own conduct as well as to another's, and moreover principles which may constitute a constraint, or limitation, upon the pursuit of one's own interests. There are, of course, other aspects of having a morality: the acknowledgement of moral principles must show itself in accepting a reference to them as reasons for limiting one's claims, in acknowledging the burden of providing a special explanation, or excuse, when one acts contrary to them, or else in showing shame and remorse and a desire to make amends, and so on. It is sufficient to remark here that having a morality is analogous to having made a firm commitment in advance; for one must acknowledge the principles of morality even when to one's disadvantage. A man whose moral judgments always coincided with his interests could be suspected of having no morality at all.

Thus the two parts of the foregoing account are intended to mirror the kinds of circumstances in which questions of justice arise and the constraints which having a morality would impose upon persons so situated. In this way one can see how the acceptance of the principles of justice might come about, for given all these conditions as described, it would be natural if the two principles of justice were to be acknowledged. Since there is no way for anyone to win special advantages for himself, each might consider it reasonable to acknowledge equality as an initial principle. There is, however, no reason why they should regard this position as final; for if there are inequalities which satisfy the second principle, the immediate gain which equality would allow can be considered as intelligently invested in view of its future return. If, as is quite likely, these inequalities work as incentives to draw out better efforts, the members of this society may look upon them as concessions to human nature: they, like us, may think that people ideally should want to serve one another. But as they are mutually self-interested, their acceptance of these inequalities is merely the acceptance of the relations in which they actually stand, and a recognition of the motives which lead them to engage in their common practices. *They* have no title to complain of one another. And so provided that the conditions of the principle are met, there is no reason why they should not allow such inequalities. Indeed, it would be short-sighted of them to do so, and could result, in most cases, only from their being dejected by the bare knowledge, or perception, that others are better situated. Each person will, however, insist on an advantage to himself, and so on a common advantage, for none is willing to sacrifice anything for the others.

These remarks are not offered as a rigorous proof that persons conceived and situated as the conjectural account supposes, and required to adopt the procedure described, would settle on the two principles of justice. For such a proof a more elaborate and formal argument would have to be given: there remain certain details to be filled in, and various alternatives to be ruled out. The argument should, however, be taken as a proof, or a sketch of a proof; for the proposition I seek to establish is a necessary one, that is, it is intended as a theorem: namely, that when mutually self-interested and rational persons confront one another in typical circumstances of justice, and when they are required by a procedure expressing the constraints of having a morality to jointly acknowledge principles by which their claims on the design of their common practices are to be judged, they will settle on these two principles as restrictions governing the assignment of rights and duties, and thereby accept them as limiting their rights against one another. It is this theorem which accounts for these principles as principles of justice, and explains how they come to be associated with this moral concept. Moreover, this theorem is analogous to those about human conduct in other branches of social thought. That is, a simplified situation is described in which rational persons pursuing certain ends and related to one another in a definite way, are required to act subject to certain limitations; then, given this situation, it is shown that they will act in a certain manner. Failure so to act would imply that one or more of the assumptions does not obtain. The foregoing account aims to establish, or to sketch, a theorem in this sense; the aim of the argument is to show the basis for saying that the principles of justice may be regarded as those principles which arise when the constraints of having a morality are imposed upon rational persons in typical circumstances of justice.

4

These ideas are, of course, connected with a familiar way of thinking about justice which goes back at least to the Greek Sophists, and which regards the acceptance of the principles of justice as a compromise between persons of roughly equal power who would enforce their will on each other if they could, but who, in view of the equality of forces amongst them and for the sake of their own peace and security acknowledge certain forms of conduct in so far as prudence seems to require. Justice is thought of as a pact between rational egoists the stability of which is dependent on a balance of power and a similarity of circumstances. While the previous account is connected with this tradition, and with its most recent variant, the theory of games, it differs from it in several important respects which, to forestall misinterpretations, I will set out here.

First, I wish to use the previous conjectural account of the background of justice as a way of analysing the concept. I do not want, therefore, to be interpreted as assuming a general theory of human motivation: when I suppose that the parties are mutually self-interested, and are not willing to have their (substantial) interests sacrificed to others, I am referring to their conduct and motives as they are taken for granted in cases where questions of justice ordinarily arise. Justice is the virtue of practices where there are assumed to be competing interests and conflicting claims, and where it is supposed that persons will press their rights on each other. That persons are mutually self-interested in certain situations and for certain purposes is what gives rise to the question of justice in practices covering those circumstances. Amongst an association of saints, if such a community could really exist, the disputes about justice could hardly occur; for they would all work selflessly together for one end, the glory of God as defined by their common religion, and reference to this end would settle every question of right. The justice of practices does not come up until there are several different parties (whether we think of these as individuals, associations, or nations and so on, is irrelevant) who do press their claims on one another, and who do regard themselves as representatives of interests which deserve to be considered. Thus the previous account involves no general theory of human motivation. Its intent is simply to incorporate into the conception of justice the relations of men to one another which set the stage for questions of justice. It makes no difference how wide or general these relations are, as this matter does not bear on the analysis of the concept.

Again, in contrast to the various conceptions of the social contract, the several parties do not establish any particular society or practice; they do not covenant to obey a particular sovereign body or to accept a given constitution. Nor do they, as in the theory of games (in certain respects a marvelously sophisticated development of this tradition), decide on individual strategies adjusted to their respective circumstances in the game. What the parties do is to *jointly* acknowledge certain *principles* of appraisal relating to their common *practices* either as already established or merely proposed. They accede to standards of judgment, not to a given practice; they do not make any specific agreement, or bargain, or adopt a particular strategy. The subject of their acknowledgement is, therefore, very general indeed; it is simply the acknowledgement of certain principles of judgment, fulfilling certain general conditions, to be used in criticizing the arrangement of their common affairs. The relations of mutual self-interest between the parties who are similarly circumstanced mirror the conditions under which questions of justice arise, and the procedure by which the principles of judgment are proposed and acknowledged reflects the constraints of having a morality. Each aspect, then, of the preceding hypothetical account serves the purpose of bringing out a feature of the notion of justice. One could, if one liked, view the principles of justice as the "solution" of this highest order "game" of adopting, subject to the procedure described, principles of argument for all coming particular "games" whose peculiarities one can in no way foresee. But this comparison, while no doubt helpful, must not obscure the fact that this highest order "game" is of a special sort.[4] Its significance is that its various pieces represent aspects of the concept of justice.

Finally, I do not, of course, conceive the several parties as necessarily coming together to establish their common practices for the first time. Some institutions may, indeed, be set up *de novo;* but I have framed the preceding account so that it will apply when the full complement of social institutions already exists and represents the result of a long period of development. Nor is the account in any way fictitious. In any society where people reflect on their institutions they will have an idea of what principles of justice would be acknowledged under the conditions described, and there will be occasions when questions of justice are actually discussed in this way. Therefore if their practices do not accord with

[4] The difficulty one gets into by a mechanical application of the theory of games to moral philosophy can be brought out by considering among several possible examples, R. B. Braithwaite's study, *Theory of Games as a Tool for the Moral Philosopher* (Cambridge, 1955). What is lacking is the concept of morality, and it must be brought into the conjectural account in some way or other. In the text this is done by the form of the procedure whereby principles are proposed and acknowledged (Section 3). If one starts directly with the particular case as known, and if one accepts as given and definitive the preferences and relative positions of the parties, whatever they are, it is impossible to give an analysis of the moral concept of fairness.

these principles, this will affect the quality of their social relations. For in this case there will be some recognized situations wherein the parties are mutually aware that one of them is being forced to accept what the other would concede is unjust. The foregoing analysis may then be thought of as representing the actual quality of relations between persons as defined by practices accepted as just. In such practices the parties will acknowledge the principles on which it is constructed, and the general recognition of this fact shows itself in the absence of resentment and in the sense of being justly treated. Thus one common objection to the theory of the social contract, its apparently historical and fictitious character, is avoided.

5

That the principles of justice may be regarded as arising in the manner described illustrates an important fact about them. Not only does it bring out the idea that justice is a primitive moral notion in that it arises once the concept of morality is imposed on mutually self-interested agents similarly circumstanced, but it emphasizes that, fundamental to justice, is the concept of fairness which relates to right dealing between persons who are cooperating with or competing against one another, as when one speaks of fair games, fair competition, and fair bargains. The question of fairness arises when free persons, who have no authority over one another, are engaging in a joint activity and amongst themselves settling or acknowledging the rules which define it and which determine the respective shares in its benefits and burdens. A practice will strike the parties as fair if none feels that, by participating in it, they or any of the others are taken advantage of, or forced to give in to claims which they do not regard as legitimate. This implies that each has a conception of legitimate claims which he thinks it reasonable for others as well as himself to acknowledge. If one thinks of the principles of justice as arising in the manner described, then they do define this sort of conception. A practice is just or fair, then, when it satisfies the principles which those who participate in it could propose to one another for mutual acceptance under the aforementioned circumstances. Persons engaged in a just, or fair, practice can face one another openly and support their respective positions, should they appear questionable, by reference to principles which it is reasonable to expect each to accept.

It is this notion of the possibility of mutual acknowledgement of principles by free persons who have no authority over one another which makes the concept of fairness fundamental to justice. Only if such acknowledgement is possible can there be true community between persons in their common practices; otherwise their relations will appear to them as founded to some extent on force. If, in ordinary speech, fairness applies more particularly to practices in which there is a choice whether to engage or not (*e.g.* in games, business competition), and justice to practices in which there is no choice (*e.g.* in slavery), the element of necessity does not render the conception of mutual acknowledgement inapplicable, although it may make it much more urgent to change unjust than unfair institutions. For one activity in which one can always engage is that of proposing and acknowledging principles to one another supposing each to be similarly circumstanced; and to judge practices by the principles so arrived at is to apply the standard of fairness to them.

Now if the participants in a practice accept its rules as fair, and so have no complaint to lodge against it, there arises a prima facie duty (and a corresponding prima facie right) of the parties to each other to act in accordance with the practice when it falls upon them to comply. When any number of persons engage in a practice, or conduct a joint undertaking according to rules, and thus restrict their liberty, those who have submitted to these restrictions when required have the right to a similar acquiescence on the part of those who have benefited by their submission. These conditions will obtain if a practice is correctly acknowledged to be fair, for in this case all who participate in it will benefit from it. The rights and duties so arising are special rights and duties in that they depend on previous actions voluntarily undertaken, in this case on the parties having engaged in a common practice and knowingly accepted its benefits.[5] It is not, however, an obligation which presupposes a deliberate performative act in the sense of a promise, or contract, and the like. An unfortunate mistake of proponents of the idea of the social contract was to suppose that political obli-

[5] For the definition of this prima facie duty, and the idea that it is a special duty, I am indebted to H. L. A. Hart. See his paper "Are There Any Natural Rights?," *Philosophical Review,* LXIV (1955), pp. 185 f.

gation does require some such act, or at least to use language which suggests it. It is sufficient that one has knowingly participated in and accepted the benefits of a practice acknowledged to be fair. This prima facie obligation may, of course, be overridden: it may happen, when it comes one's turn to follow a rule, that other considerations will justify not doing so. But one cannot, in general, be released from this obligation by denying the justice of the practice only when it falls on one to obey. If a person rejects a practice, he should, so far as possible, declare his intention in advance, and avoid participating in it or enjoying its benefits.

This duty I have called that of fair play, but it should be admitted that to refer to it in this way is, perhaps, to extend the ordinary notion of fairness. Usually acting unfairly is not so much the breaking of any particular rule, even if the infraction is difficult to detect (cheating), but taking advantage of loop-holes or ambiguities in rules, availing oneself of unexpected or special circumstances which make it impossible to enforce them, insisting that rules be enforced to one's advantage when they should be suspended, and more generally, acting contrary to the intention of a practice. It is for this reason that one speaks of the sense of fair play: acting fairly requires more than simply being able to follow rules; what is fair must often be felt, or perceived, one wants to say. It is not, however, an unnatural extension of the duty of fair play to have it include the obligation which participants who have knowingly accepted the benefits of their common practice owe to each other to act in accordance with it when their performance falls due; for it is usually considered unfair if someone accepts the benefits of a practice but refuses to do his part in maintaining it. Thus one might say of the tax-dodger that he violates the duty of fair play: he accepts the benefits of government but will not do his part in releasing resources to it; and members of labor unions often say that fellow workers who refuse to join are being unfair: they refer to them as "free riders," as persons who enjoy what are the supposed benefits of unionism, higher wages, shorter hours, job security, and the like, but who refuse to share in its burdens in the form of paying dues, and so on.

The duty of fair play stands beside other prima facie duties such as fidelity and gratitude as a basic moral notion; yet it is not to be confused with them. These duties are all clearly distinct, as would be obvious from their definitions. As with any moral duty, that of fair play implies a constraint on self-interest in particular cases; on occasion it enjoins conduct which a rational egoist strictly defined would not decide upon. So while justice does not require of anyone that he sacrifice his interests in that *general position* and procedure whereby the principles of justice are proposed and acknowledged, it may happen that in particular situations, arising in the context of engaging in a practice, the duty of fair play will often cross his interests in the sense that he will be required to forego particular advantages which the peculiarities of his circumstances might permit him to take. There is, of course, nothing surprising in this. It is simply the consequence of the firm commitment which the parties may be supposed to have made, or which they would make, in the general position, together with the fact that they have participated in and accepted the benefits of a practice which they regard as fair.

Now the acknowledgement of this constraint in particular cases, which is manifested in acting fairly or wishing to make amends, feeling ashamed, and the like, when one has evaded it, is one of the forms of conduct by which participants in a common practice exhibit their recognition of each other as persons with similar interests and capacities. In the same way that, failing a special explanation, the criterion for the recognition of suffering is helping one who suffers, acknowledging the duty of fair play is a necessary part of the criterion for recognizing another as a person with similar interests and feelings as oneself.[6] A person who never under any circumstances showed a wish to help others in pain would show, at the same time, that he did not recognize that they were in pain; nor could he have any feelings of affection or friendship for anyone; for having these feelings implies, failing special circumstances, that he comes to their aid when they are suffering. Recognition that another is a person in pain shows itself in sympathetic action; this primitive natural response of compassion is one of those responses upon which the various forms of moral conduct are built.

Similarly, the acceptance of the duty of fair play by participants

[6] I am using the concept of criterion here in what I take to be Wittgenstein's sense. That the response of compassion, under appropriate circumstances, is part of the criterion for whether or not a person understands what "pain" means, is, I think, in the *Philosophical Investigations*. The view in the text is simply an extension of this idea. I cannot, however, attempt to justify it here.

in a common practice is a reflection in each person of the recognition of the aspirations and interests of the others to be realized by their joint activity. Failing a special explanation, their acceptance of it is a necessary part of the criterion for their recognizing one another as persons with similar interests and capacities, as the conception of their relations in the general position supposes them to be. Otherwise they would show no recognition of one another as persons with similar capacities and interests, and indeed, in some cases perhaps hypothetical, they would not recognize one another as persons at all, but as complicated objects involved in a complicated activity. To recognize another as a person one must respond to him and act towards him in certain ways; and these ways are intimately connected with the various prima facie duties. Acknowledging these duties in *some* degree, and so having the elements of morality, is not a matter of choice, or of intuiting moral qualities, or a matter of the expression of feelings or attitudes (the three interpretations between which philosophical opinion frequently oscillates); it is simply the possession of one of the forms of conduct in which the recognition of others as persons is manifested.

These remarks are unhappily obscure. Their main purpose here, however, is to forestall, together with the remarks in Section 4, the misinterpretation that, on the view presented, the acceptance of justice and the acknowledgement of the duty of fair play depends in every day life solely on there being a *de facto* balance of forces between the parties. It would indeed be foolish to underestimate the importance of such a balance in securing justice; but it is not the only basis thereof. The recognition of one another as persons with similar interests and capacities engaged in a common practice must, failing a special explanation, show itself in the acceptance of the principles of justice and the acknowledgement of the duty of fair play.

The conception at which we have arrived, then, is that the principles of justice may be thought of as arising once the constraints of having a morality are imposed upon rational and mutually self-interested parties who are related and situated in a special way. A practice is just if it is in accordance with the principles which all who participate in it might reasonably be expected to propose or to acknowledge before one another when they are similarly circumstanced and required to make a firm commitment in advance without knowledge of what will be their peculiar condition, and thus when it meets standards which the parties could accept as fair should occasion arise for them to debate its merits. Regarding the participants themselves, once persons knowingly engage in a practice which they acknowledge to be fair and accept the benefits of doing so, they are bound by the duty of fair play to follow the rules when it comes their turn to do so, and this implies a limitation on their pursuit of self-interest in particular cases.

Now one consequence of this conception is that, where it applies, there is no moral value in the satisfaction of a claim incompatible with it. Such a claim violates the conditions of reciprocity and community amongst persons, and he who presses it, not being willing to acknowledge it when pressed by another, has no grounds for complaint when it is denied; whereas he against whom it is pressed can complain. As it cannot be mutually acknowledged it is a resort to coercion; granting the claim is possible only if one party can compel acceptance of what the other will not admit. But it makes no sense to concede claims the denial of which cannot be complained of in preference to claims the denial of which can be objected to. Thus in deciding on the justice of a practice it is not enough to ascertain that it answers to wants and interests in the fullest and most effective manner. For if any of these conflict with justice, they should not be counted, as their satisfaction is no reason at all for having a practice. It would be irrelevant to say, even if true, that it resulted in the greatest satisfaction of desire. In tallying up the merits of a practice one must toss out the satisfaction of interests the claims of which are incompatible with the principles of justice.

6

The discussion so far has been excessively abstract. While this is perhaps unavoidable, I should now like to bring out some of the features of the conception of justice as fairness by comparing it with the conception of justice in classical utilitarianism as represented by Bentham and Sidgwick, and its counterpart in welfare economics. This conception assimilates justice to benevolence and the latter in turn to the most efficient design of institutions to promote the general welfare. Justice is a kind of efficiency.

Now it is said occasionally that this form of utilitarianism puts no restrictions on what might be a just assignment of rights and duties in that there might be circumstances which, on utilitarian grounds, would justify institutions highly offensive to our ordinary sense of justice. But the classical utilitarian conception is not totally unprepared for this objection. Beginning with the notion that the general happiness can be represented by a social utility function consisting of a sum of individual utility functions with identical weights (this being the meaning of the maxim that each counts for one and no more than one), it is commonly assumed that the utility functions of individuals are similar in all essential respects. Differences between individuals are ascribed to accidents of education and upbringing, and they should not be taken into account. This assumption, coupled with that of diminishing marginal utility, results in a prima facie case for equality, for example, of equality in the distribution of income during any given period of time, laying aside indirect effects on the future. But even if utilitarianism is interpreted as having such restrictions built into the utility function, and even if it is supposed that these restrictions have in practice much the same result as the application of the principles of justice (and appear, perhaps, to be ways of expressing these principles in the language of mathematics and psychology), the fundamental idea is very different from the conception of justice as fairness. For one thing, that the principles of justice should be accepted is interpreted as the contingent result of a higher order administrative decision. The form of this decision is regarded as being similar to that of an entrepreneur deciding how much to produce of this or that commodity in view of its marginal revenue, or to that of someone distributing goods to needy persons according to the relative urgency of their wants. The choice between practices is thought of as being made on the basis of the allocation of benefits and burdens to individuals (these being measured by the present capitalized value of their utility over the full period of the practice's existence), which results from the distribution of rights and duties established by a practice.

Moreover, the individuals receiving these benefits are not conceived as being related in any way: they represent so many different directions in which limited resources may be allocated. The value of assigning resources to one direction rather than another depends solely on the preferences and interests of individuals as individuals.

The satisfaction of desire has its value irrespective of the moral relations between persons, say as members of a joint undertaking, and of the claims which, in the name of these interests, they are prepared to make on one another:[7] and it is this value which is to be taken into account by the (ideal) legislator who is conceived as adjusting the rules of the system from the center so as to maximize the value of the social utility function.

It is thought that the principles of justice will not be violated by a legal system so conceived provided these executive decisions are correctly made. In this fact the principles of justice are said to have their derivation and explanation; they simply express the most important general features of social institutions in which the administrative problem is solved in the best way. These principles have, indeed, a special urgency because, given the facts of human nature, so much depends on them; and this explains the peculiar quality of the moral feelings associated with justice. This assimilation of justice to a higher order executive decision, certainly a striking conception, is central to classical utilitarianism; and it also brings out its profound individualism, in one sense of this ambiguous word. It regards persons as so many *separate* directions in which benefits and burdens may be assigned; and the value of the satisfaction or dissatisfaction of desire is not thought to depend in any way on the moral relations in which individuals stand, or on the kinds of claims which they are willing, in the pursuit of their interests, to press on each other.

[7] An idea essential to the classical utilitarian conception of justice. Bentham is firm in his statement of it. (*The Principles of Morals and Legislation,* Chap. II, sec. iv. See also Chap. X, sec. x, footnote 1.) The same point is made in *The Limits of Jurisprudence Defined,* pp. 115 f. Although much recent welfare economics, as found in such important works as I. M. D. Little, *A Critique of Welfare Economics,* 2nd ed. (Oxford, 1957) and K. J. Arrow, *Social Choice and Individual Values* (New York, 1951), dispenses with the idea of cardinal utility, and use instead the theory of ordinal utility as stated by J. R. Hicks, *Value and Capital,* 2nd ed. (Oxford, 1946), Part I, it assumes with utilitarianism that individual preferences have value as such, and so accepts the idea being criticized here. I hasten to add, however, that this is no objection to it as a means of analysing economic policy, and for that purpose it may, indeed, be a necessary simplifying assumption. Nevertheless it is an assumption which cannot be made in so far as one is trying to analyse moral concepts, especially the concept of justice, as economists would, I think, agree. Justice is usually regarded as a separate and distinct part of any comprehensive criterion of economic policy. See, for example, Tibor Scitovsky, *Welfare and Competition* (London, 1952), pp. 59–69, and Little, *op. cit.,* Chap. VII.

7

Many social decisions are, of course, of an administrative nature. Certainly this is so when it is a matter of social utility in what one may call its ordinary sense: that is, when it is a question of the efficient design of social institutions for the use of common means to achieve common ends. In this case either the benefits and burdens may be assumed to be impartially distributed, or the question of distribution is misplaced, as in the instance of maintaining public order and security or national defence. But as an interpretation of the basis of the principles of justice, classical utilitarianism is mistaken. It *permits* one to argue, for example, that slavery is unjust on the grounds that the advantages to the slaveholder as slaveholder do not counterbalance the disadvantages to the slave and to society at large burdened by a comparatively inefficient system of labour. Now the conception of justice as fairness, when applied to the practice of slavery with its offices of slaveholder and slave, would not allow one to consider the advantages of the slaveholder in the first place. As that office is not in accordance with principles which could be mutually acknowledged, the gains accruing to the slaveholder, assuming them to exist, cannot be counted as in *any* way mitigating the injustice of the practice. The question whether these gains outweigh the disadvantages to the slave and to society cannot arise, since in considering the justice of slavery these gains have no weight at all which requires that they be overridden. Where the conception of justice as fairness applies, slavery is *always* unjust.

I am not, of course, suggesting the absurdity that the classical utilitarians approved of slavery. I am only rejecting a type of argument which their view allows them to use in support of their disapproval of it. The conception of justice as derivative from efficiency implies that judging the justice of a practice is always, in principle at least, a matter of weighing up advantages and disadvantages, each having an intrinsic value or disvalue as the satisfaction of interests, irrespective of whether or not these interests necessarily involve acquiescence in principles which could not be mutually acknowledged. Utilitarianism cannot account for the fact that slavery is always unjust, nor for the fact that it would be recognized as irrelevant in defeating the accusation of injustice for one person to say to another, engaged with him in a common practice and debating its merits, that nevertheless it allowed of the greatest satisfaction of desire. The charge of injustice cannot be rebutted in this way. If justice were derivative from a higher order executive efficiency, this would not be so.

But now, even if it is taken as established that, so far as the ordinary conception of justice goes, slavery is always unjust (that is, slavery by definition violates commonly recognized principles of justice), the classical utilitarian would surely reply that these principles, as other moral principles subordinate to that of utility, are only generally correct. It is simply for the most part true that slavery is less efficient than other institutions; and while common sense may define the concept of justice so that slavery is unjust, nevertheless, where slavery would lead to the greatest satisfaction of desire, it is not wrong. Indeed, it is then right, and for the very same reason that justice, as ordinarily understood, is usually right. If, as ordinarily understood, slavery is always unjust, to this extent the utilitarian conception of justice might be admitted to differ from that of common moral opinion. Still the utilitarian would want to hold that, as a matter of moral principle, his view is correct in giving no special weight to considerations of justice beyond that allowed for by the general presumption of effectiveness. And this, he claims, is as it should be. The everyday opinion is morally in error, although, indeed, it is a useful error, since it protects rules of generally high utility.

The question, then, relates not simply to the analysis of the concept of justice as common sense defines it, but the analysis of it in the wider sense as to how much weight considerations of justice, as defined, are to have when laid against other kinds of moral considerations. Here again I wish to argue that reasons of justice have a *special* weight for which only the conception of justice as fairness can account. Moreover, it belongs to the concept of justice that they do have this special weight. While Mill recognized that this was so, he thought that it could be accounted for by the special urgency of the moral feelings which naturally support principles of such high utility. But it is a mistake to resort to the urgency of feeling; as with the appeal to intuition, it manifests a failure to pursue the question far enough. The special weight of considerations of justice can be explained from the conception of justice as fairness. It is only necessary to elaborate a bit what has already been said as follows.

If one examines the circumstances in which a certain tolerance of slavery is justified, or perhaps better, excused, it turns out that these are of a rather special sort. Perhaps slavery exists as an inheritance from the past and it proves necessary to dismantle it piece by piece; at times slavery may conceivably be an advance on previous institutions. Now while there may be some excuse for slavery in special conditions, it is never an excuse for it that it is sufficiently advantageous to the slaveholder to outweigh the disadvantages to the slave and to society. A person who argues in this way is not perhaps making a wildly irrelevant remark; but he is guilty of a moral fallacy. There is disorder in his conception of the ranking of moral principles. For the slaveholder, by his own admission, has no moral title to the advantages which he receives as a slaveholder. He is no more prepared than the slave to acknowledge the principle upon which is founded the respective positions in which they both stand. Since slavery does not accord with principles which they could mutually acknowledge, they each may be supposed to agree that it is unjust: it grants claims which it ought not to grant and in doing so denies claims which it ought not to deny. Amongst persons in a general position who are debating the form of their common practices, it cannot, therefore, be offered as a reason for a practice that, in conceding these very claims that ought to be denied, it nevertheless meets existing interests more effectively. By their very nature the satisfaction of these claims is without weight and cannot enter into any tabulation of advantages and disadvantages.

Furthermore, it follows from the concept of morality that, to the extent that the slaveholder recognizes his position *vis-à-vis* the slave to be unjust, he would not choose to press his claims. His not wanting to receive his special advantages is one of the ways in which he shows that he thinks slavery is unjust. It would be fallacious for the legislator to suppose, then, that it is a ground for having a practice that it brings advantages greater than disadvantages, if those for whom the practice is designed, and to whom the advantages flow, acknowledge that they have no moral title to them and do not wish to receive them.

For these reasons the principles of justice have a special weight;

and with respect to the principle of the greatest satisfaction of desire, as cited in the general position amongst those discussing the merits of their common practices, the principles of justice have an absolute weight. In this sense they are not contingent; and this is why their force is greater than can be accounted for by the general presumption (assuming that there is one) of the effectiveness, in the utilitarian sense, of practices which in fact satisfy them.

If one wants to continue using the concepts of classical utilitarianism, one will have to say, to meet this criticism, that at least the individual or social utility functions must be so defined that no value is given to the satisfaction of interests the representative claims of which violate the principles of justice. In this way it is no doubt possible to include these principles within the form of the utilitarian conception; but to do so is, of course, to change its inspiration altogether as a moral conception. For it is to incorporate within it principles which cannot be understood on the basis of a higher order executive decision aiming at the greatest satisfaction of desire.

It is worth remarking, perhaps, that this criticism of utilitarianism does not depend on whether or not the two assumptions, that of individuals having similar utility functions and that of diminishing marginal utility, are interpreted as psychological propositions to be supported or refuted by experience, or as moral and political principles expressed in a somewhat technical language. There are, certainly, several advantages in taking them in the latter fashion. For one thing, one might say that this is what Bentham and others really meant by them, at least as shown by how they were used in arguments for social reform. More importantly, one could hold that the best way to defend the classical utilitarian view is to interpret these assumptions as moral and political principles. It is doubtful whether, taken as psychological propositions, they are true of men in general as we know them under normal conditions. On the other hand, utilitarians would not have wanted to propose them merely as practical working principles of legislation, or as expedient maxims to guide reform, given the egalitarian sentiments of modern society. When pressed they might well have invoked the idea of a more or less equal capacity of men in relevant respects if given an equal chance in a just society. But if the argument above regarding slavery is correct, then granting these assumptions as moral and political principles makes no difference. To view individuals as equally fruitful lines for the allocation of benefits, even as a matter of moral principle, still leaves the mistaken notion that the satisfaction of desire has value in itself irrespective of the relations between persons as members of a common practice, and irrespective of the claims upon one another which the satisfaction of interests represents. To see the error of this idea one must give up the conception of justice as an executive decision altogether and refer to the notion of justice as fairness: that participants in a common practice be regarded as having an original and equal liberty and that their common practices be considered unjust unless they accord with principles which persons so circumstanced and related could freely acknowledge before one another, and so could accept as fair. Once the emphasis is put upon the concept of the mutual recognition of principles by participants in a common practice the rules of which are to define their several relations and give form to their claims on one another, then it is clear that the granting of a claim the principle of which could not be acknowledged by each in the general position (that is, in the position in which the parties propose and acknowledge principles before one another) is not a reason for adopting a practice. Viewed in this way, the background of the claim is seen to exclude it from consideration; that it can represent a value in itself arises from the conception of individuals as separate lines for the assignment of benefits, as isolated persons who stand as claimants on an administrative or benevolent largesse. Occasionally persons do so stand to one another; but this is not the general case, nor, more importantly, is it the case when it is a matter of the justice of practices themselves in which participants stand in various relations to be appraised in accordance with standards which they may be expected to acknowledge before one another. Thus however mistaken the notion of the social contract may be as history, and however far it may overreach itself as a general theory of social and political obligation, it does express, suitably interpreted, an essential part of the concept of justice.

8

By way of conclusion I should like to make two remarks: first, the original modification of the utilitarian principle (that it require of practices that the offices and positions defined by them be equal unless it is reasonable to suppose that the representative man in *every* office would find the inequality to his advantage), slight as it may appear at first sight, actually has a different conception of justice standing behind it. I have tried to show how this is so by developing the concept of justice as fairness and by indicating how this notion involves the mutual acceptance, from a general position, of the principles on which a practice is founded, and how this in turn requires the exclusion from consideration of claims violating the principles of justice. Thus the slight alteration of principle reveals another family of notions, another way of looking at the concept of justice.

Second, I should like to remark also that I have been dealing with the *concept* of justice. I have tried to set out the kinds of principles upon which judgments concerning the justice of practices may be said to stand. The analysis will be successful to the degree that it expresses the principles involved in these judgments when made by competent persons upon deliberation and reflection.[8] Now every people may be supposed to have the concept of justice, since in the life of every society there must be at least some relations in which the parties consider themselves to be circumstanced and related as the concept of justice as fairness requires. Societies will differ from one another not in having or in failing to have this notion but in the range of cases to which they apply it and in the emphasis which they give to it as compared with other moral concepts.

A firm grasp of the concept of justice itself is necessary if these variations, and the reasons for them, are to be understood. No

[8] For a further discussion of the idea expressed here, see my paper, "Outline of a Decision Procedure for Ethics," in the *Philosophical Review*, LX (1951), pp. 177–97. For an analysis, similar in many respects but using the notion of the ideal observer instead of that of the considered judgment of a competent person, see Roderick Firth, "Ethical Absolutism and the Ideal Observer," *Philosophy and Phenomenological Research*, XII (1952), pp. 317–45. While the similarities between these two discussions are more important than the differences, an analysis based on the notion of a considered judgment of a competent person, as it is based on a kind of judgment, may prove more helpful in understanding the features of moral judgment than an analysis based on the notion of an ideal observer, although this remains to be shown. A man who rejects the conditions imposed on a considered judgment of a competent person could no longer profess to *judge* at all. This seems more fundamental than his rejecting the conditions of observation, for these do not seem to apply, in an ordinary sense, to making a moral judgment.

study of the development of moral ideas and of the differences between them is more sound than the analysis of the fundamental moral concepts upon which it must depend. I have tried, therefore, to give an analysis of the concept of justice which should apply generally, however large a part the concept may have in a given morality, and which can be used in explaining the course of men's thoughts about justice and its relations to other moral concepts. How it is to be used for this purpose is a large topic which I cannot, of course, take up here. I mention it only to emphasize that I have been dealing with the concept of justice itself and to indicate what use I consider such an analysis to have.

BRIAN BARRY

Reflections on "Justice as Fairness"

. . . Rawls suggests that the principles of just distribution are those principles which would be agreed on by rational, self-interested men, "sufficiently equal in power and ability to guarantee that in normal circumstances none is able to dominate the others" (p. 82), as providing a basis upon which they would be willing to have their common affairs regulated in perpetuity.

Rawls does not, I think, ever devote much space to proving that the principles agreed on in such circumstances would be properly described as principles of *justice;* still less that justice should be defined in those terms. In "Justice as Fairness" he says that "The character and respective situations of the parties [*e.g.* their egoism and their equal strength] reflect . . . the fact that questions of justice arise when conflicting claims are made upon the design of a practice and where it is taken for granted that each person will insist, as far as possible, on what he considers his rights." At the same time, "The procedure whereby principles are proposed and acknowledged represents constraints, analogous to those of having a morality;" for "having a morality must at least imply the acknowledgement of principles as impartially applying to one's own conduct as well as to another's, and moreover principles which may constitute a constraint, or limitation, upon the pursuit of one's own interests." (p. 83.)

Brian Barry, "On Social Justice," *The Oxford Review* (Trinity Term, 1967), pp. 33–43 (with omissions). Reprinted by permission of the author. References in the text to "Justice as Fairness" have been altered so as to refer to the pagination in this volume.

The required conclusion is not, however, established by these points. What Rawls needs to show is that, if the procedure he describes were employed in the kind of situation he describes, the principles agreed on would necessarily be principles of justice. This does not follow from the passage I have quoted, which maintains only that the problem of justice arises in situations such as those he describes and that the procedure he describes automatically produces the impartiality and limitation of interest-seeking which is a minimum condition of morality. A situation in which interests conflict is no doubt relevant to justice, but it is equally relevant to all the other principles by which social relationships may be ordered; and to say that a procedure guarantees a minimum condition of morality is not the same as saying that it produces the particular set of moral principles embodied in the concept of justice.

Rawls could avoid this criticism (though at the cost of opening another line of attack) by saying that he was simply proposing to appropriate the word "justice" to refer to whatever principles would be agreed on in the situation that he depicts. But he does not take this course, for he writes that "justice is to be understood in its customary sense as representing but *one* of the many virtues of social institutions," and claims that the principles which would be chosen in the prescribed set-up are "typical of a family of principles normally associated with the concept of justice." (p. 77.) Rawls' case is, then, that certain principles would be chosen by rational self-interested men who were forced to agree, on equal terms, to the principle that should govern their relations in future; and that these principles would in fact be recognizable as falling under our ordinary concept of justice. This does not of course entail that they should fit our ordinary concept at every point; but that we would be prepared to regard them as constituting a "rational reconstruction" of our ordinary concept, a more coherent, streamlined form of it, which we should be willing to adopt in its place. Thus, the next step is to see what principles Rawls believes *would* be adopted; and to ask (a) whether there is a good case for thinking they would be adopted, (b) whether, in any case, they coincide at all closely with our ordinary concept of justice, and (c) whether, even if they do not, they are still valuable principles.

III

As far as I know, nobody has actually tried the experiment of setting up the Rawlsian initial conditions and finding out what principles emerged. Rawls does not rely on empirical evidence; but if someone challenged him with some he might reply that he is speaking of *rational* men, and if the experimental results do not agree with his own conclusions this merely shows that the subjects employed were not fully rational. Rawls' method, then, is deductive. If Martians play chess then we at once know, without any information about Martians, that a good move in Martian chess is also a good move in Earth chess. Similarly, provided that Martians have conflicting interests which they desire to pursue, they will (if Rawls is right) agree on the same principles for regulating their affairs as human beings will, insofar as they are rational in pursuing those interests.

According to Rawls, two principles would be agreed upon: "first, each person participating in a practice, or affected by it, has an equal right to the most extensive liberty compatible with a like liberty for all; and second, inequalities are arbitrary unless it is reasonable to expect that they will work out to everyone's advantage, and provided the positions and offices to which they attach, or from which they may be gained, are open to all." (p. 78.) The basic idea is fairly simple, though its working out can become very complicated. In order to decide what would be a just distribution, the participants in any practice start from a baseline of equality: this means a situation where there is equality in the "benefits and burdens attached to [different offices and positions] either directly or indirectly, such as prestige and wealth, or liability to taxation and compulsory services." (p. 79.) They then ask, taking this equal position as a point of comparison, whether there is any possible system of inequalities which would make everybody better off—and that means *everybody*. "The representative man in every office or position defined by a practice, when he views it as a going concern, must find it reasonable to prefer his condition and prospects with the inequality to what they would be under the practice without it. The principle excludes, therefore, the justification of inequalities on the grounds that the disadvantages of those in one position are outweighed by the greater advantages of those in another position." (p. 80.)

Let us now take up the first question: would these principles be adopted by rational, self-interested men? Two kinds of objection might, I think, be pressed. I shall call them the practical and the theoretical objection. The practical difficulty is that the ordinary uncertainty of the future is not so great that men putting forward principles for the regulation of things in the future might not be able to make a shrewd guess about their chances of being near the top or near the bottom in a system of inequalities. Thus, Rawls assumes too easily that because of uncertainty men would have to leave out of account their own positions in putting forward principles. I call this a practical difficulty because it can be eliminated by making the initial conditions stronger. As before, we can simply add the postulate that the men (or, if you like, beings) who are choosing the principles are suffering from a temporary amnesia about their personal qualities, etc.; and that all they know is that they have conflicting interests but the possibility of gains from co-operation. Rawls does not take this line of retreat in "Justice as Fairness" but he has done so since.[1] Obviously, adding this condition emphasizes the abstract, deductive nature of the whole operation, but given Rawls' purposes it seems to me a legitimate way of clearing an irrelevant practical difficulty out of the way.

The other objection I call the theoretical one because it challenges the deduction at its core. The objection is that, no matter how perfectly the initial conditions are set up, rational self-interested men would *not* necessarily choose the Rawlsian principles, because there is no good reason why they should do so. This criticism centres round Rawls' second principle: that inequalities are to be accepted if and only if they can be expected to make the worst-off person under them better-off than he would have been under a regime of absolute equality. It is important to see exactly how Rawls arrives at the conclusion that this principle would meet with universal approval among anonymous, self-interested beings—that is to say, beings who know they have interests they wish to pursue, even though they do not know what these interests are. Rawls writes that the principles each man puts forward

[1] See his "Constitutional Liberty and the Concept of Justice," *Nomos VI.*

"will express the conditions in accordance with which each is the least unwilling to have his interests limited in the design of practices, given the competing interests of the others, on the supposition that interests of others will be limited likewise. *The restrictions which would so arise might be thought of as those a person would keep in mind if he were designing a practice in which his enemy were to assign him his place.*" (p. 83; my italics.)

Now, if the sentence I have italicized is right, it must be allowed that Rawls' deduction works. A man whose place is to be assigned him by his enemy will obviously concentrate on designing the system of distributions so that the worst-off position will be as pleasant as possible. He knows that he can, and must, concentrate on this and ignore everything else, because he knows for certain that, whatever the worst-off position is, he will be occupying it. But our hypothetical principle-choosers are *not* going to be assigned their positions by their enemy. They know in fact that the allocation of places will depend (in proportions that they do not know) on personal characteristics and on luck. And since they do not at the moment remember what personal characteristics they have, they can simply regard positions as allocated by a random process.

Now the question is, if you know that outcomes are determined by a random process (or, more generally, by a process which is not directed at giving you personally one outcome rather than another) is it rational to behave as if the outcome were going to be determined by the wishes of your enemy? This is the vexed problem of decision-making under conditions of uncertainty. Rawls' solution has been put forward often as the maximin criterion: "maximin" simply refers to the fact that it prescribes the choice which *maximizes* the *minimum* pay-off. In other words, the decision-maker looks at the possible consequences of each alternative to discover the worst possible outcome that each could produce. For each alternative he asks: if everything went wrong, how catastrophic would it be? And he then picks the alternative which gives him the smallest losses if everything goes wrong. Clearly this is a play-safe strategy, a conservative strategy. Does it make sense as a universal response to uncertainty?

Let us consider a simple example. Either it will rain today or the sun will shine; and I can either take my raincoat or leave it at home. If the sun shines and I have left my raincoat, I shall be very pleased; on the other hand, if I leave my raincoat and it rains, I shall be very annoyed. If I take my raincoat and it rains, I shall be fairly pleased in that I am at least suitably clad, though less pleased than the combination of sun and no raincoat would make me; if the sun shines when I take my raincoat, I shall be somewhat annoyed, though less annoyed than I would be at having to walk through the rain without a raincoat.

The maximin criterion dictates that I take my raincoat: the worst that can happen is that the sun will shine; and this is less annoying than the worst thing that can happen if I leave my raincoat behind, namely get wet. This would obviously be the right plan if I were convinced that there was a Weather Man who took a malicious pleasure in thwarting me. But if I thought that "someone up there likes me" and was striving to make me as happy as possible, I would be more sensible to adopt a maximax policy: instead of choosing the best of the worst outcomes I would go for the best of the best outcomes. In the present case, this would entail that I leave my raincoat behind and trust in providence to make the sun shine, for my most pleasant outcome consists of the combination of no raincoat and the sun shining.

Suppose, however, that I don't believe that my decision about taking a raincoat or not will have any effect on whether it rains or whether the sun shines. How should I decide then which to do? The natural answer would seem to be that I should try to guess how likely it is to rain and should act accordingly. If there is a fair chance of its raining, I take my coat; if I think the chance of rain is very remote, I leave it behind. Exactly how likely rain has to be before it is worth taking my coat depends on the relative pleasantness and unpleasantness of the four possible outcomes and my taste for risk-taking. Fortunately, there is no need for the present purpose to go into details. The essential point is that almost anyone would think it sensible to go out without a raincoat if the probability of rainfall is below *some* level; but on the maximin criterion one would always take a raincoat if there was any chance of rain at all, however remote. The conclusion to be drawn is, I suggest, that it is not rational to follow the maximin policy except where someone *is* responding to your choices in such a way as to damage you. In other cases some sort of system for playing the percentages is more rational.

The implications for Rawls' construction are plain. It is not legitimate to say that rational self-interest requires the adoption of a maximin policy. It follows that there would not be agreement on the second of Rawls' principles. Rational choosers would look not just at the minimum but at the average and the spread around it. They would then pick a set of principles which would lead to a high average level of well-being; whether they would prefer one with more equal or less equal distribution would depend on their taste for gambling.[2]

IV

Although the two Rawlsian principles cannot be deduced from Rawls' initial conditions, they are still worth examining in their own right, first, as principles of *justice,* and, second, as principles of *distribution* in general. For, if they either embody or replace the ordinary criteria of social justice, the optimistic view that a single formula can be produced will have been vindicated—provided, of course, that we are willing to accept a single formula in two parts; and I think we ought to be, so long as the two parts are completely consistent with one another.

Rawls' two principles do not, I suggest, correspond with the main elements in the ordinary notion of justice. The first principle, that some reason has to be given for treating people unequally, is no doubt a constituent part of the concept of justice; but this is because it is a necessary condition of bringing different people's claims into a moral relationship with one another. It is not connected with justice in particular. The second principle falls into two parts: the maximin criterion and the prescription that "positions and offices" carrying privileges should be "open to all." (p. 78). The latter part, if interpreted to mean that such positions should be open to those most fully qualified, is fairly clearly relevant to justice, though it seems oddly limited in scope to occur in a general formula for justice. The original and controversial first part seems not to be a principle of justice at all. If it were followed, the results might quite often coincide with those required by justice, but where they did not, I do not think we would be inclined to adopt the maximin criterion and drop other conceptions.

[2] See William Vickrey, "Utility, Strategy and Social Decision Rules," *The Quarterly Journal of Economics,* LXXIV.

The only ground on which one can defend an inequality as just, in Rawls' conception, is that introducing it will lead to the worst off member of the society being better off than he would otherwise have been. I should like to suggest, however, that, although this would often be a good reason for saying the inequality was *justified,* it would never be a good reason for calling it *just.* For justice is not a forward-looking virtue. Justice consists in some appropriate relationship between what a person has done or what he is now and the benefits that he receives or the costs that he bears. The size of incentive payments is not determined by the criteria of just distribution. It may be considered essential to pay someone a certain amount in order to get him to do something and it may also be considered vital that he should do it. But the payment does not automatically become just when these two conditions obtain. It would be perfectly comprehensible to assert that it was unjust for anyone to be paid so much "rent" for the exercise of the talent in question, but that it was right in this instance for justice to give way to public interest.

If we assume (as we have in the last example) that Rawls' maximin criterion is to be applied in a society where people are allocated to jobs and have to be got to work in them by inducements, differentials may tend to be too large for justice. But there is nothing in Rawls' formula specifying that it should be applied in a "liberal" society. People might be allocated to jobs and kept at work in them by coercion: that is to say, instead of being made better off than the norm by doing what is wanted they are made worse off than the norm if they don't do what is wanted. Under such conditions, exact equality could be maintained. Unpleasantness of work would have to be compensated for to *maintain* equality but, even so, it might be thought that justice had been infringed in the other direction from that in which a liberal society deviated. Of course, a "liberal" could argue that a directive-coercive system is so much less efficient than a liberal system that, not only would the best off under a liberal system be better off than anyone under a directive-coercive system, but even the *worst* off person in a "liberal" system would be better off than anybody in a directive-coercive system. This may be true; then again it may not. And in any case it seems to me dubious to suppose that the justice of all differentials turns on the results of such an experiment.

V

The reader may have become impatient with the latest phase of the discussion. I imagine him saying: "All right, the maximin criterion doesn't correspond to the ordinary notion of justice, and we don't particularly want to give up the ordinary notion of justice. But (as you admitted in the incentive-payment example) we are willing to allow justice in this ordinary sense to be overridden. Doesn't the maximin criterion provide an acceptable overriding principle?" This is a very attractive idea, and maybe there will be some people who are prepared to stick to the maximin principle through thick and thin. I should like, however, to suggest that there is a certain arbitrary quality about it, compared with a frank recognition of multiple "ultimate" principles with no simple rule for settling clashes between them.

Rawls tells us that "in deciding on the justice of a practice it is not enough to ascertain that it answers to wants and interests in the fullest and most effective manner. For if any of these conflict with justice, they should not be counted, as their satisfaction is *no reason at all.* It would be irrelevant to say, even if true, that it resulted in the greatest satisfaction of desire. In tallying up the *merits* of a practice one must toss out the satisfaction of interests the claims of which are incompatible with the principle of justice." (p. 93, my italics.) The expressions I have italicized show how weak is the form of moral pluralism that Rawls is willing to accept, compared with what he appeared to be offering us when he said that justice is only one possible virtue of institutions. The claim that an institution satisfies wants more fully than any alternative is "no reason at all" in favour of it—irrelevant to its "merits"—if it conflicts with the requirements of justice. "With respect to the principle of the greatest satisfaction of desire . . . the principles of justice have an absolute weight." (p. 99.) Against this view, I should like to suggest that utilitarian considerations cannot simply be "tossed out" when they conflict with the criteria of justice. I shall argue this in connection with Rawls' criteria of justice, but I think the same argument could be made against the absolute priority of any distributive criteria.

I have argued above that someone rationally pursuing his own self-interest would not accept the inflexibility of the maximin criterion; and that he would insist on taking account of the whole range of positions, not just the lowest. Similarly here I wish to argue that a responsible moral agent should not commit himself to giving an absolute priority to the principles of justice, but that he should allow for the possibility that a large increase in utility might counter-balance a small decrease in justice. In terms of the maximin criterion this means that it is possible to conceive a situation in which it would be morally justifiable for someone to say: "I know I'm better off than you; but I think you ought to do so-and-so because it would be of great benefit to me and only a minor inconvenience to you." For example, suppose that one of us drives a Bentley and the other a Mini; and that we have to decide which of us is to get the big garage and which of us the small one. On Rawls' principles it might be concluded that the man with the Mini should be compensated with the big garage and the Bentley left to stand outside (since it won't go in the small garage). But this seems absurd. At the very least it does not seem unreasonable to prefer, say, a large gain for the better off and a smaller gain for the worse off to an infinitesimally larger gain for the worse off and a loss for the better off—provided that these are the only alternatives.

I have followed Rawls in taking up the problem of conflicts between the maximin criterion and the principle of maximizing the satisfaction of wants, and I have suggested that it would not be desirable for the latter always to override the former. But there are other principles that can conflict with the maximin criterion, and here too one might well be uneasy in assenting to the universal priority of the maximin criterion. One of these is the notion of "desert." In arguing earlier that the maximin criterion did not coincide with the ordinary notion of justice it was the strong connection between desert and justice that I had in mind. Here, of course, we are not concerned with whether the maximin criterion is properly regarded as a principle of justice but with whether it is appropriate to treat it as an overriding principle when making moral judgments about social institutions. I do not think that desert can be written off. A survey whose findings were published recently illustrates the strong hold that desert seems to have over people, in this country at least.[3] Respondents were asked, among

[3] *New Society,* April 6th, 1967, page 492. Acknowledgement is made to the Opinion Research Centre and to the Editor of *New Society* for permission to quote the findings cited below.

other things, which of three criteria for earned incomes they thought "most important." Almost half (49%) said "that people with special skills are fully rewarded," as against 41% saying "that lowest paid workers get a reasonable wage" and 10% "that incomes become more equal." And the replies to another question show vividly that the support for "fully rewarding" those with "special skills" was derived from a belief in desert—an intrinsically proper relationship between the work done and its reward—rather than a forward-looking attempt to attract labour to jobs where it was needed. For when asked "which two of these [five possible reasons] do you think are the best reasons for a pay rise?" very few respondents (16%) gave the "incentive" answer: "It's difficult to find people for the job." The most popular two reasons (especially among Conservatives and Liberals but getting a clear majority of votes among Labour supporters too) were the two most clearly tied to hierarchical notions of desert: "it's a responsible job" (61%) and "it's a job which needs long training" (56%). Two less hierarchical bases of ascribing desert—"long hours" and "difficult job"—came a long way behind in third and fourth places (27% and 21%) leaving the need to attract labour sharing last place with the principle of comparability ("other people doing similar work get more pay"). Ours is a society in which the elite are rewarded not only with deference but with hard cash—and most people seem to think that is the way it should be.

I shall not pursue this line of argument any further, since either one of the criteria for judgement mentioned—the utilitarian one and that of desert—is sufficient to break the primacy of the maximin criterion if one accepts that in case of conflict one of these might be followed in preference to the maximin criterion. Before leaving this criterion, however, I should like to say a few words in its defence. One may concede (as I wish to do) that it is not a principle of justice and that it is not an overriding principle of morality. One may concede further (as again I would wish to do) that it is not an ultimate principle at all. This does not prevent one from recognizing its attraction as one possible compromise point between two ultimate principles, namely the utilitarian principle and the principle of equality. The strength of the maximin criterion lies in its promise of providing a determinate point of compromise. The only other way of reaching a compromise is to ask how much of one value is worth how much of the other, and these weightings are in the nature of the case almost impossible to formulate in general terms.

We can present the point most conveniently in a simple illustrative diagram.

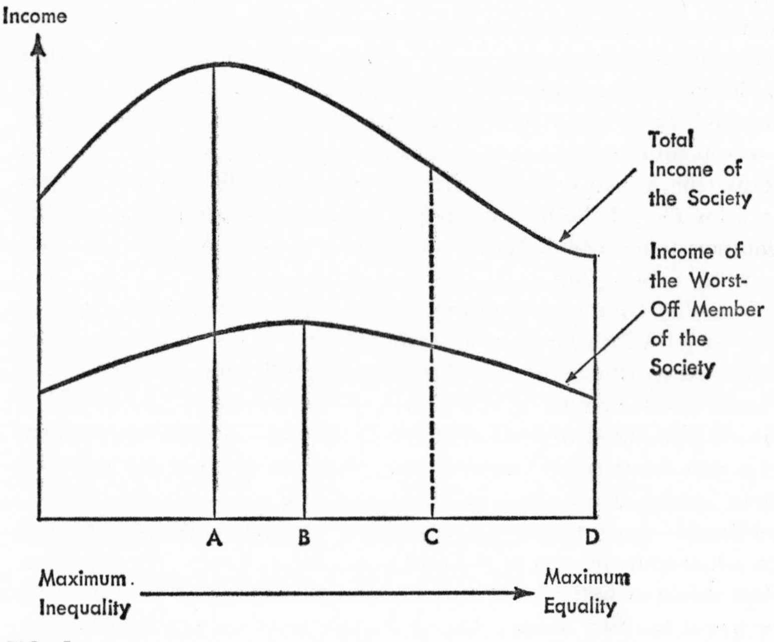

FIG. 1

As the equality of distribution increases, from the minimum on the left to the maximum on the right, we suppose that the total income of all those concerned (added together) first rises and then falls, and that the income of the worst-off follows the same pattern but reaches a maximum at a more egalitarian point. These seem reasonable assumptions. Now, the two simple maximizing prescriptions, taken separately, yield definite results. If we want to maximize total income we adopt A, and if we want to maximize equality we adopt D. But suppose we don't want to go overboard on either; then what point should we adopt? Rawls' maximin criterion provides a prescription which is both in effect a compromise between equality and total income and yet at the same time gives a definite result. According to this we maximize the income of the worst-off and thus adopt B. Of course, this is not the only possible compromise position; of the many possible alternatives, one somewhat more egalitarian solution is represented by C. But whereas B can be read off the diagram as the point at which the curve turns down, C depends on looking at all feasible combinations of the two amounts—equality and total income—and the judgement that the most desirable combination attainable is to be found at that point. This can be expressed technically by noting that whereas the determination of the points A, B and D does not depend on the scale—the height of the curves could be doubled or halved without altering the results—the position of C does depend crucially on the scale, since it is two amounts that are being weighed against one another and not merely one amount being maximized.

Thus, where the main considerations which are taken to be relevant to some question happen to be those of equal distribution and total income (or, less specifically, "general utility"), the maximin principle provides a determinate compromise position—it can be put forward with a certain plausibility as the point beyond which it is not "reasonable" to push equality. A good example of this may be drawn from the equalization of wages and salaries. In a recent article, Professor H. A. Clegg has suggested that a movement towards "the redistribution of earned incomes" might be achieved by the use of a national minimum wage.[4] The question then arises, on what basis should the level of this minimum wage be fixed? And the answer that appears to be given is: the level that maximizes the pay of the lowest paid. For Clegg writes: "The consequence of a £15 minimum would be a surge in wage-costs and prices which would benefit no one, *not even the lowest-paid;* but a minimum of £10 10*s*. or £11 should not be unmanageable." (My italics.)

[4] See "The Case for a National Minimum Wage," *The London Times*, March 28th, 1967, p. 9.

. . . .

BERNARD A. O. WILLIAMS

The Idea of Equality

The idea of equality is used in political discussion both in statements of fact, or what purport to be statements of fact—that men *are* equal—and in statements of political principles or aims—that men *should be* equal, as at present they are not. The two can be, and often are, combined: the aim is then described as that of securing a state of affairs in which men are treated as the equal beings which they in fact already are, but are not already treated as being. In both these uses, the idea of equality notoriously encounters the same difficulty: that on one kind of interpretation the statements in which it figures are much too strong, and on another kind much too weak, and it is hard to find a satisfactory interpretation that lies between the two.[1]

To take first the supposed statement of fact: it has only too often been pointed out that to say that all men are equal in all those characteristics in respect of which it makes sense to say that men are equal or unequal, is a patent falsehood; and even if some more restricted selection is made of these characteristics, the statement does not look much better. Faced with this obvious objection, the defender of the claim that all men are equal is likely to offer a weaker interpretation. It is not, he may say, in their

B. A. O. Williams, "The Idea of Equality," in Peter Laslett and W. G. Runciman, eds., *Philosophy, Politics and Society*, Series II, pp. 110–131.

[1] For an illuminating discussion of this and related questions, see R. Wollheim and I. Berlin, "Equality," *Proceedings of the Aristotelian Society*, LVI (1955–6), p. 281 seq.

skill, intelligence, strength or virtue that men are equal, but merely in their being men: it is their common humanity that constitutes their equality. On this interpretation, we should not seek for some special characteristics in respect of which men are equal, but merely remind ourselves that they are all men. Now to this it might be objected that being men is not a respect in which men can strictly speaking be said to be *equal;* but, leaving that aside, there is the more immediate objection that if all that the statement does is to remind us that men are men, it does not do very much, and in particular does less than its proponents in political argument have wanted it to do. What looked like a paradox has turned into a platitude.

I shall suggest in a moment that even in this weak form the statement is not so vacuous as this objection makes it seem; but it must be admitted that when the statement of equality ceases to claim more than is warranted, it rather rapidly reaches the point where it claims less than is interesting. A similar discomfiture tends to overcome the practical maxim of equality. It cannot be the aim of this maxim that all men should be treated alike in all circumstances, or even that they should be treated alike as much as possible. Granted that, however, there is no obvious stopping point before the interpretation which makes the maxim claim only that men should be treated alike in similar circumstances; and since "circumstances" here must clearly include reference to what a man is, as well as to his purely external situation, this comes very much to saying that for every difference in the way men are treated, some general reason or principle of differentiation must be given. This may well be an important principle; some indeed have seen in it, or in something very like it, an essential element of morality itself.[2] But it can hardly be enough to constitute the principle that was advanced in the name of *equality*. It would be in accordance with this principle, for example, to treat black men differently from others just because they were black, or poor men differently just because they were poor, and this cannot accord with anyone's idea of equality.

In what follows I shall try to advance a number of considerations that can help to save the political notion of equality from

[2] For instance, R. M. Hare: see his *Language of Morals,* Oxford: The Clarendon Press, 1952.

these extremes of absurdity and of triviality. These considerations are in fact often employed in political argument, but are usually bundled together into an unanalysed notion of equality in a manner confusing to the advocates, and encouraging to the enemies, of that ideal. These considerations will not enable us to define a distinct third interpretation of the statements which use the notion of equality; it is rather that they enable us, starting with the weak interpretations, to build up something that in practice can have something of the solidity aspired to by the strong interpretations. In this discussion, it will not be necessary all the time to treat separately the supposedly factual application of the notion of equality, and its application in the maxim of action. Though it is sometimes important to distinguish them, and there are clear grounds for doing so, similar considerations often apply to both. The two go significantly together: on the one hand, the point of the supposedly factual assertion is to back up social ideals and programmes of political action; on the other hand—a rather less obvious point, perhaps—those political proposals have their force because they are regarded not as gratuitously egalitarian, aiming at equal treatment for reasons, for instance, of simplicity or tidiness, but as affirming an equality which is believed in some sense already to exist, and to be obscured or neglected by actual social arrangements.

1. Common humanity. The factual statement of men's equality was seen, when pressed, to retreat in the direction of merely asserting the equality of men as men; and this was thought to be trivial. It is certainly insufficient, but not, after all, trivial. That all men are human is, if a tautology, a useful one, serving as a reminder that those who belong anatomically to the species *homo sapiens*, and can speak a language, use tools, live in societies, can interbreed despite racial differences, etc., are also alike in certain other respects more likely to be forgotten. These respects are notably the capacity to feel pain, both from immediate physical causes and from various situations represented in perception and in thought; and the capacity to feel affection for others, and the consequences of this, connected with the frustration of this affection, loss of its objects, etc. The assertion that men are alike in the possession of these characteristics is, while indisputable and (it may be) even necessarily true, not trivial. For it is certain that there are political

and social arrangements that systematically neglect these characteristics in the case of some groups of men, while being fully aware of them in the case of others; that is to say, they treat certain men as though they did not possess these characteristics, and neglect moral claims that arise from these characteristics and which would be admitted to arise from them.

Here it may be objected that the mere fact that ruling groups in certain societies treat other groups in this way does not mean that they neglect or overlook the characteristics in question. For, it may be suggested, they may well recognize the presence of these characteristics in the worse-treated group, but claim that in the case of that group, the characteristics do not give rise to any moral claim; the group being distinguished from other members of society in virtue of some further characteristic (for instance, by being black), this may be cited as the ground of treating them differently, whether they feel pain, affection, etc., or not.

This objection rests on the assumption, common to much moral philosophy that makes a sharp distinction between fact and value, that the question whether a certain consideration is *relevant* to a moral issue is an evaluative question: to state that a consideration is relevant or irrelevant to a certain moral question is, on this view, itself to commit oneself to a certain kind of moral principle or outlook. Thus, in the case under discussion, to say (as one would naturally say) that the fact that a man is black is, by itself, quite irrelevant to the issue of how he should be treated in respect of welfare, etc., would, on this view, be to commit oneself to a certain sort of moral principle. This view, taken generally, seems to me quite certainly false. The principle that men should be differentially treated in respect of welfare merely on grounds of their colour is not a special sort of moral principle, but (if anything) a purely arbitrary assertion of will, like that of some Caligulan ruler who decided to execute everyone whose name contained three "R"s.

This point is in fact conceded by those who practice such things as colour discrimination. Few can be found who will explain their practice merely by saying, "But they're black: and it is my moral principle to treat black men differently from others." If any reasons are given at all, they will be reasons that seek to correlate the fact of blackness with certain other considerations which are at least candidates for relevance to the question of how a man should be treated: such as insensitivity, brute stupidity, ineducable irresponsibility, etc. Now these reasons are very often rationalizations, and the correlations claimed are either not really believed, or quite irrationally believed, by those who claim them. But this is a different point; the argument concerns what counts as a moral reason, and the rationalizer broadly agrees with others about what counts as such—the trouble with him is that his reasons are dictated by his policies, and not conversely. The Nazis' "anthropologists" who tried to construct theories of Aryanism were paying, in very poor coin, the homage of irrationality to reason.

The question of relevance in moral reasons will arise again, in a different connexion, in this paper. For the moment its importance is that it gives a force to saying that those who neglect the moral claims of certain men that arise from their human capacity to feel pain, etc., are *overlooking* or *disregarding* those capacities; and are not just operating with a special moral principle, conceding the capacities to these men, but denying the moral claim. Very often, indeed, they have just persuaded themselves that the men in question have those capacities in a lesser degree. Here it is certainly to the point to assert the apparent platitude that these men are also human.

I have discussed this point in connexion with very obvious human characteristics of feeling pain and desiring affection. There are, however, other and less easily definable characteristics universal to humanity, which may all the more be neglected in political and social arrrangements. For instance, there seems to be a characteristic which might be called "a desire for self-respect;" this phrase is perhaps not too happy, in suggesting a particular culturally-limited, bourgeois value, but I mean by it a certain human desire to be identified with what one is doing, to be able to realize purposes of one's own, and not to be the instrument of another's will unless one has willingly accepted such a role. This is a very inadequate and in some ways rather empty specification of a human desire; to a better specification, both philosophical reflection and the evidences of psychology and anthropology would be relevant. Such investigations enable us to understand more deeply, in respect of the desire I have gestured towards and of similar characteristics, what it is to be human; and of what it is to be human, the apparently trivial statement of men's equality as men can serve as a reminder.

2. Moral capacities. So far we have considered respects in which men can be counted as all alike, which respects are, in a sense, negative: they concern the capacity to suffer, and certain needs that men have, and these involve men in moral relations as the recipients of certain kinds of treatment. It has certainly been a part, however, of the thought of those who asserted that men were equal, that there were more positive respects in which men were alike: that they were equal in certain things that they could do or achieve, as well as in things that they needed and could suffer. In respect of a whole range of abilities, from weight lifting to the calculus, the assertion is, as was noted at the beginning, not plausible, and has not often been supposed to be. It has been held, however, that there are certain other abilities, both less open to empirical test and more essential in moral connexions, for which it is true that men are equal. These are certain sorts of moral ability or capacity, the capacity for virtue or achievement of the highest kind of moral worth.

The difficulty with this notion is that of identifying any purely moral capacities. Some human capacities are more relevant to the achievement of a virtuous life than others: intelligence, a capacity for sympathetic understanding, and a measure of resoluteness would generally be agreed to be so. But these capacities can all be displayed in non-moral connexions as well, and in such connexions would naturally be thought to differ from man to man like other natural capacities. That this is the fact of the matter has been accepted by many thinkers, notably, for instance, by Aristotle. But against this acceptance, there is a powerful strain of thought that centres on a feeling of ultimate and outrageous absurdity in the idea that the achievement of the highest kind of moral worth should depend on natural capacities, unequally and fortuitously distributed as they are; and this feeling is backed up by the observation that these natural capacities are not themselves the bearers of the moral worth, since those that have them are as gifted for vice as for virtue.

This strain of thought has found many types of religious expression; but in philosophy it is to be found in its purest form in Kant. Kant's view not only carries to the limit the notion that moral worth cannot depend on contingencies, but also emphasizes, in its picture of the Kingdom of Ends, the idea of *respect* which is owed to each man as a rational moral agent—and, since men are equally such agents, is owed equally to all, unlike admiration and similar attitudes, which are commanded unequally by men in proportion to their unequal possession of different kinds of natural excellence. These ideas are intimately connected in Kant, and it is not possible to understand his moral theory unless as much weight is given to what he says about the Kingdom of Ends as is always given to what he says about duty.

The very considerable consistency of Kant's view is bought at what would generally be agreed to be a very high price. The detachment of moral worth from all contingencies is achieved only by making man's characteristic as a moral or rational agent a transcendental characteristic; man's capacity to will freely as a rational agent is not dependent on any empirical capacities he may have—and, in particular, is not dependent on empirical capacities which men may possess unequally—because, in the Kantian view, the capacity to be a rational agent is not itself an empirical capacity at all. Accordingly, the respect owed equally to each man as a member of the Kingdom of Ends is not owed to him in respect of any empirical characteristics that he may possess, but solely in respect of the transcendental characteristic of being a free and rational will. The ground of the respect owed to each man thus emerges in the Kantian theory as a kind of secular analogue of the Christian conception of the respect owed to all men as equally children of God. Though secular, it is equally metaphysical: in neither case is it anything empirical *about* men that constitutes the ground of equal respect.

This transcendental, Kantian conception cannot provide any solid foundation for the notions of equality among men, or of equality of respect owed to them. Apart from the general difficulties of such transcendental conceptions, there is the obstinate fact that the concept of "moral agent," and the concepts allied to it such as that of responsibility, do and must have an empirical basis. It seems empty to say that all men are equal as moral agents, when the question, for instance, of men's responsibility for their actions is one to which empirical considerations are clearly relevant, and one which moreover receives answers in terms of different degrees of responsibility and different degrees of rational control over action. To hold a man responsible for his actions is presumably the central case of treating him as a moral agent, and if men are not treated as equally responsible, there is not much left to their equality as moral agents.

If, without its transcendental basis, there is not much left to men's equality as moral agents, is there anything left to the notion of the *respect* owed to all men? This notion of "respect" is both complex and unclear, and I think it needs, and would repay, a good deal of investigation. Some content can, however, be attached to it; even if it is some way away from the ideas of moral agency. There certainly is a distinction, for instance, between regarding a man's life, actions or character from an æsthetic or technical point of view, and regarding them from a point of view which is concerned primarily with what it is *for him* to live that life and do those actions in that character. Thus from the technological point of view, a man who has spent his life in trying to make a certain machine which could not possibly work is merely a failed inventor, and in compiling a catalogue of those whose efforts have contributed to the sum of technical achievement, one must "write him off": the fact that he devoted himself to this useless task with constant effort and so on, is merely irrelevant. But from a human point of view, it is clearly not irrelevant: we are concerned with him, not merely as "a failed inventor," but as a man who wanted to be a successful inventor. Again, in professional relations and the world of work, a man operates, and his activities come up for criticism, under a variety of professional or technical titles, such as "miner" or "agricultural labourer" or "junior executive." The technical or professional attitude is that which regards the man solely under that title, the human approach that which regards him as *a man who has* that title (among others), willingly, unwillingly, through lack of alternatives, with pride, etc.

That men should be regarded from the human point of view, and not merely under these sorts of titles, is part of the content that might be attached to Kant's celebrated injunction "treat each man as an end in himself, and never as a means only." But I do not think that this is all that should be seen in this injunction, or all that is concerned in the notion of "respect." What is involved in the examples just given could be explained by saying that each man is owed an effort at identification: that he should not be regarded as the surface to which a certain label can be applied, but one should try to see the world (including the label) from his point of view. This injunction will be based on, though not of course fully explained by, the notion that men are conscious beings who necessarily have intentions and purposes and see what they are doing in a certain light. But there seem to be further injunctions connected with the Kantian maxim, and with the notion of "respect," that go beyond these considerations. There are forms of exploiting men or degrading them which would be thought to be excluded by these notions, but which cannot be excluded merely by considering how the exploited or degraded men see the situation. For it is precisely a mark of extreme exploitation or degradation that those who suffer it do *not* see themselves differently from the way they are seen by the exploiters; either they do not see themselves as anything at all, or they acquiesce passively in the role for which they have been cast. Here we evidently need something more than the precept that one should respect and try to understand another man's consciousness of his own activities; it is also that one may not suppress or destroy that consciousness.

All these I must confess to be vague and inconclusive considerations, but we are dealing with a vague notion: one, however, that we possess, and attach value to. To try to put these matters properly in order would be itself to try to reach conclusions about several fundamental questions of moral philosophy. What we must ask here is what these ideas have to do with equality. We started with the notion of men's equality as moral agents. This notion appeared unsatisfactory, for different reasons, in both an empirical and a transcendental interpretation. We then moved, *via* the idea of "respect," to the different notion of regarding men not merely under professional, social or technical titles, but with consideration of their own views and purposes. This notion has at least this much to do with equality: that the titles which it urges us to look behind are the conspicuous bearers of social, political and technical *inequality*, whether they refer to achievement (as in the example of the inventor), or to social roles (as in the example of work titles). It enjoins us not to let our fundamental attitudes to men be dictated by the criteria of technical success or social position, and not to take them at the value carried by these titles and by the structures in which these titles place them. This does not mean, of course, that the more fundamental view that should be taken of men is in the case of every man the same: on the contrary. But it does mean that each man is owed the effort of understanding, and that in achieving it, each man is to be (as it were) abstracted from certain conspicuous structures of inequality in which we find him.

These injunctions are based on the proposition that men are beings who are necessarily to some extent conscious of themselves and of the world they live in. (I omit here, as throughout the discussion, the clinical cases of people who are mad or mentally defective, who always constitute special exceptions to what is in general true of men.) This proposition does not assert that men are equally conscious of themselves and of their situation. It was precisely one element in the notion of exploitation considered above that such consciousness can be decreased by social action and the environment; we may add that it can similarly be increased. But men are at least potentially conscious, to an indeterminate degree, of their situation and of what I have called their "titles," are capable of reflectively standing back from the roles and positions in which they are cast; and this reflective consciousness may be enhanced or diminished by their social condition.

It is this last point that gives these considerations a particular relevance to the political aims of egalitarianism. The mere idea of regarding men from "the human point of view," while it has a good deal to do with politics, and a certain amount to do with equality, has nothing specially to do with political equality. One could, I think, accept this as an ideal, and yet favour, for instance, some kind of hierarchical society, so long as the hierarchy maintained itself without compulsion, and there was human understanding between the orders. In such a society, each man would indeed have a very conspicuous title which related him to the social structure; but it might be that most people were aware of the human beings behind the titles, and found each other for the most part content, or even proud, to have the titles that they had. I do not know whether anything like this has been true of historical hierarchical societies; but I can see no inconsistency in someone's espousing it as an ideal, as some (influenced in many cases by a sentimental picture of the Middle Ages) have done. Such a person would be one who accepted the notion of "the human view," the view of each man as something more than his title, as a valuable ideal, but rejected the ideals of political equality.

Once, however, one accepts the further notion that the degree of man's consciousness about such things as his role in society is itself in some part the product of social arrangements, and that it can be increased, this ideal of a stable hierarchy must, I think, disappear. For what keeps stable hierarchies together is the idea of necessity, that it is somehow foreordained or inevitable that there should be these orders; and this idea of necessity must be eventually undermined by the growth of people's reflective consciousness about their role, still more when it is combined with the thought that what they and the others have always thought about their roles in the social system was the product of the social system itself.

It might be suggested that a certain man who admitted that people's consciousness of their roles was conditioned in this way might nevertheless believe in the hierarchical ideal: but that in order to preserve the society of his ideal, he would have to make sure that the idea of the conditioning of consciousness did not get around to too many people, and that their consciousness about their roles did not increase too much. But such a view is really a very different thing from its naïve predecessor. Such a man, no longer himself "immersed" in the system, is beginning to think in terms of compulsion, the deliberate *prevention* of the growth of consciousness, which is a poisonous element absent from the original ideal. Moreover, his attitude (or that of rulers similar to himself) towards the other people in the ideal society must now contain an element of condescension or contempt, since he will be aware that their acceptance of what they suppose to be necessity is a delusion. This is alien to the spirit of human understanding on which the original ideal was based. The hierarchical idealist cannot escape the fact that certain things which can be done decently without self-consciousness can, with self-consciousness, be done only hypocritically. This is why even the rather hazy and very general notions that I have tried to bring together in this section contain some of the grounds of the ideal of political equality.

3. EQUALITY IN UNEQUAL CIRCUMSTANCES. The notion of equality is invoked not only in connexions where men are claimed in some sense all to be equal, but in connexions where they are agreed to be unequal, and the question arises of the distribution of, or access to, certain goods to which their inequalities are relevant. It may be objected that the notion of equality is in fact misapplied in these connexions, and that the appropriate ideas are those of

fairness or justice, in the sense of what Aristotle called "distributive justice," where (as Aristotle argued) there is no question of regarding or treating everyone as equal, but solely a question of distributing certain goods in proportion to men's recognized inequalities.

I think it is reasonable to say against this objection that there is some foothold for the notion of equality even in these cases. It is useful here to make a rough distinction between two different types of inequality, inequality of *need* and inequality of *merit,* with a corresponding distinction between goods—on the one hand, goods demanded by the need, and on the other, goods that can be earned by the merit. In the case of needs, such as the need for medical treatment in case of illness, it can be presumed for practical purposes that the persons who have the need actually desire the goods in question, and so the question can indeed be regarded as one of distribution in a simple sense, the satisfaction of an existing desire. In the case of merit, such as for instance the possessions of abilities to profit from a university education, there is not the same presumption that everyone who has the merit has the desire for the goods in question, though it may, of course, be the case. Moreover, the good of a university education may be legitimately, even if hopelessly, desired by those who do not possess the merit; while medical treatment or unemployment benefit are either not desired, or not legitimately desired, by those who are not ill or unemployed, that is do not have the appropriate need. Hence the distribution of goods in accordance with merit has a competitive aspect lacking in the case of distribution according to need. For these reasons, it is appropriate to speak, in the case of merit, not only of the distribution of the good, but of the distribution of the opportunity of achieving the good. But this, unlike the good itself, can be said to be distributed equally to everybody, and so one does encounter a notion of *general* equality, much vaunted in our society today, the notion of equality of opportunity.

Before considering this notion further, it is worth noticing certain resemblances and differences between the cases of need and of merit. In both cases, we encounter the matter (mentioned before in this paper) of the relevance of reasons. Leaving aside preventive medicine, the proper ground of distribution of medical care is ill health: this is a necessary truth. Now in very many societies, while ill health may work as a necessary condition of receiving treatment, it does not work as a sufficient condition, since such treatment costs money, and not all who are ill have the money; hence the possession of sufficient money becomes in fact an additional necessary condition of actually receiving treatment. Yet more extravagantly, money may work as a sufficient condition by itself, without any medical need, in which case the reasons that actually operate for the receipt of this good are just totally irrelevant to its nature; however, since only a few hypochondriacs desire treatment when they do not need it, this is, in this case, a marginal phenomenon.

When we have the situation in which, for instance, wealth is a further necessary condition of the receipt of medical treatment, we can once more apply the notions of equality and inequality: not now in connexion with the inequality between the well and the ill, but in connexion with the inequality between the rich ill and the poor ill, since we have straightforwardly the situation of those whose needs are the same not receiving the same treatment, though the needs are the ground of the treatment. This is an irrational state of affairs.

It may be objected that I have neglected an important distinction here. For, it may be said, I have treated the ill health and the possession of money as though they were regarded on the same level, as "reasons for receiving medical treatment," and this is a muddle. The ill health is, at most, a ground of the *right* to receive medical treatment; whereas the money is, in certain circumstances, the causally necessary condition of securing the right, which is a different thing. There is something in the distinction that this objection suggests: there is a distinction between a man's rights, the reasons why he should be treated in a certain way, and his power to secure those rights, the reasons why he can in fact get what he deserves. But this objection does not make it inappropriate to call the situation of inequality an "irrational" situation: it just makes it clearer what is meant by so calling it. What is meant is that it is a situation in which reasons are insufficiently *operative;* it is a situation insufficiently controlled by reasons—and hence by reason itself. The same point arises with another form of equality and equal rights, equality before the law. It may be said that in a certain society, men have equal rights to a fair trial, to seek redress from the law for wrongs committed against them, etc. But if a fair trial or redress from the law can be secured in that society only by moneyed and educated persons, to insist that everyone *has* this right, though only these particular persons can *secure* it, rings hollow to the point of cynicism: we are concerned not with the abstract existence of rights, but with the extent to which those rights govern what actually happens.

Thus when we combine the notions of the *relevance* of reasons, and the *operativeness* of reasons, we have a genuine moral weapon, which can be applied in cases of what is appropriately called unequal treatment, even where one is not concerned with the equality of people as a whole. This represents a strengthening of the very weak principle mentioned at the beginning of this paper, that for every difference in the way men are treated, a reason should be given: when one requires further that the reasons should be relevant, and that they should be socially operative, this really says something.

Similar considerations will apply to cases of merit. There is, however, an important difference between the cases of need and merit, in respect of the relevance of reasons. It is a matter of logic that particular sorts of needs constitute a reason for receiving particular sorts of good. It is, however, in general a much more disputable question whether certain sorts of merit constitute a reason for receiving certain sorts of good. For instance, let it be agreed, for the sake of argument, that the public school system provides a superior type of education, which it is a good thing to receive. It is then objected that access to this type of education is unequally distributed, because of its cost: among boys of equal promise or intelligence, only those from wealthy homes will receive it, and, indeed, boys of little promise or intelligence will receive it, if from wealthy homes; and this, the objection continues, is irrational.

The defender of the public school system might give two quite different sorts of answer to this objection; besides, that is, the obvious type of answer which merely disputes the facts alleged by the objector. One is the sort of answer already discussed in the case of need: that we may agree, perhaps, that boys of promise and intelligence have a right to a superior education, but in actual economic circumstances, this right cannot always be secured, etc. The other is more radical: this would dispute the premise of the objection that intelligence and promise are, at least by themselves, the grounds for receiving this superior type of education. While perhaps not asserting that wealth itself constitutes the ground, the defender of the system may claim that other characteristics significantly correlated with wealth are such grounds; or, again, that it is the purpose of this sort of school to maintain a tradition of leadership, and the best sort of people to maintain this will be people whose fathers were at such schools. We need not try to pursue such arguments here. The important point is that, while there can indeed be genuine disagreements about what constitutes the relevant sort of merit in such cases, such disagreements must also be disagreements about the nature of the good to be distributed. As such, the disagreements do not occur in a vacuum, nor are they logically free from restrictions. There is only a limited number of reasons for which education could be regarded as a good, and a limited number of purposes which education could rationally be said to serve; and to the limitations on this question, there correspond limitations on the sorts of merit or personal characteristic which could be rationally cited as grounds of access to this good. Here again we encounter a genuine strengthening of the very weak principle that, for differences in the way that people are treated, reasons should be given.

We may return now to the notion of equality of opportunity; understanding this in the normal political sense of equality of opportunity for *everyone in society* to secure certain goods. This notion is introduced into political discussion when there is question of the access to certain goods which, first, even if they are not desired by everyone in society, are desired by large numbers of people in all sections of society (either for themselves, or, as in the case of education, for their children), or would be desired by people in all sections of society if they knew about the goods in question and thought it possible for them to attain them; second, are goods which people may be said to earn or achieve; and third, are goods which not all the people who desire them can have. This third condition covers at least three different cases, however, which it is worth distinguishing. Some desired goods, like positions of prestige, management, etc., are *by their very nature* limited: whenever there are some people who are in command or prestigious positions, there are necessarily others who are not. Other goods are *contingently* limited, in the sense that there are certain conditions of access to them which in fact not everyone satisfies, but there is no intrinsic limit to the numbers who might gain access to it by satisfying the conditions: university education is usually regarded in this light nowadays, as something which requires certain conditions of admission to it which in fact not everyone satisfies, but which an indefinite proportion of people might satisfy. Third, there are goods which are *fortuitously* limited, in the sense that although everyone or large numbers of people satisfy the conditions of access to them, there is just not enough of them to go round; so some more stringent conditions or system of rationing have to be imposed, to govern access in an imperfect situation. A good can, of course, be both contingently and fortuitously limited at once: when, due to shortage of supply, not even the people who are qualified to have it, limited in numbers though they are, can in every case have it. It is particularly worth distinguishing those kinds of limitation, as there can be significant differences of view about the way in which a certain good is limited. While most would now agree that high education is contingently limited, a Platonic view would regard it as necessarily limited.

Now the notion of equality of opportunity might be said to be the notion that a limited good shall in fact be allocated on grounds which do not *a priori* exclude any section of those that desire it. But this formulation is not really very clear. For suppose grammar school education (a good perhaps contingently, and certainly fortuitously, limited) is allocated on grounds of ability as tested at the age of 11; this would normally be advanced as an example of equality of opportunity, as opposed to a system of allocation on grounds of parents' wealth. But does not the criterion of ability exclude *a priori* a certain section of people, namely those that are not able—just as the other excludes *a priori* those who are not wealthy? Here it will obviously be said that this was not what was meant by *a priori* exclusion: the present argument just equates this with exclusion of anybody, that is, with the mere existence of some condition that has to be satisfied. What then is *a priori* exclusion? It must mean exclusion on grounds *other* than those appropriate or rational for the good in question. But this still will not do as it stands. For it would follow from this that so long as those allocating grammar school education on grounds of wealth thought that such grounds were appropriate or rational (as they might in one of the ways discussed above in connexion with public schools), they could sincerely describe their system as one of equality of opportunity—which is absurd.

Hence it seems that the notion of equality of opportunity is more complex than it first appeared. It requires not merely that there should be no exclusion from access on grounds other than those appropriate or rational for the good in question, but that the grounds considered appropriate for the good should themselves be such that people from all sections of society have an equal chance of satisfying them. What now is a "section of society?" Clearly we cannot include under this term sections of the populace identified just by the characteristics which figure in the grounds for allocating the good—since, once more, any grounds at all must exclude some section of the populace. But what about sections identified by characteristics which are *correlated* with the grounds of exclusion? There are important difficulties here: to illustrate this, it may help first to take an imaginary example.

Suppose that in a certain society great prestige is attached to membership of a warrior class, the duties of which require great physical strength. This class has in the past been recruited from certain wealthy families only; but egalitarian reformers achieve a change in the rules, by which warriors are recruited from all sections of the society, on the results of a suitable competition. The effect of this, however, is that the wealthy families still provide virtually all the warriors, because the rest of the populace is so undernourished by reason of poverty that their physical strength is inferior to that of the wealthy and well nourished. The reformers protest that equality of opportunity has not really been achieved; the wealthy reply that in fact it has, and that the poor now have the opportunity of becoming warriors—it is just bad luck that their characteristics are such that they do not pass the test. "We are not," they might say, "excluding anyone *for* being poor; we exclude people for being weak, and it is unfortunate that those who are poor are also weak."

This answer would seem to most people feeble, and even cynical. This is for reasons similar to those discussed before in connexion with equality before the law; that the supposed equality of opportunity is quite empty—indeed, one may say that it does not really exist—unless it is made more effective than this. For one knows that it could be made more effective; one knows that there is a causal connexion between being poor and being undernourished, and between being undernourished and being physically weak. One supposes further that something could be done—subject to whatever economic conditions obtain in the imagined society—to alter the distribution of wealth. All this being so, the appeal by the wealthy to the "bad luck" of the poor must appear as disingenuous.

It seems then that a system of allocation will fall short of equality of opportunity if the allocation of the good in question in fact works out unequally or disproportionately between different sections of society, if the unsuccessful sections are under a disadvantage which could be removed by further reform or social action. This was very clear in the imaginary example that was given, because the causal connexions involved are simple and well known. In actual fact, however, the situations of this type that arise are more complicated, and it is easier to overlook the causal connexions involved. This is particularly so in the case of educational selection, where such slippery concepts as "intellectual ability" are involved. It is a known fact that the system of selection for grammar schools by the "11+" examination favours children in direct proportion to their social class, the children of professional homes having proportionately greater success than those from working class homes. We have every reason to suppose that these results are the product, in good part, of environmental factors; and we further know that imaginative social reform, both of the primary educational system and of living conditions, would favourably affect those environmental factors. In these circumstances, this system of educational selection falls short of equality of opportunity.[3]

This line of thought points to a connexion between the idea of equality of opportunity, and the idea of equality of persons, which is stronger than might at first be suspected. We have seen that one is not really offering equality of opportunity to Smith and Jones if one contents oneself with applying the same criteria to Smith and Jones at, say, the age of 11; what one is doing there is to apply the same criteria to Smith as affected by favourable conditions and to Jones as affected by unfavourable but curable conditions. Here there is a necessary pressure to equal up the conditions: to give *Smith* and *Jones* equality of opportunity involves regarding their conditions, where curable, as themselves part of what is done to Smith and Jones, and not part of Smith and Jones themselves. Their identity, for these purposes, does not include their curable environment, which is itself unequal and a contributor of inequality.

[3] See on this C. A. R. Crosland, "Public Schools and English Education," *Encounter,* July 1961.

This abstraction of persons in themselves from unequal environments is a way, if not of regarding them as equal, at least of moving recognizably in that direction; and is itself involved in equality of opportunity.

One might speculate about how far this movement of thought might go. The most conservative user of the notion of equality of opportunity is, if sincere, prepared to abstract the individual from some effects of his environment. We have seen that there is good reason to press this further, and to allow that the individuals whose opportunities are to be equal should be abstracted from more features of social and family background. Where should this stop? Should it even stop at the boundaries of heredity? Suppose it were discovered that when all curable environmental disadvantages had been dealt with, there was a residual genetic difference in brain constitution, for instance, which was correlated with differences in desired types of ability; but that the brain constitution could in fact be changed by an operation.[4] Suppose further that the wealthier classes could afford such an operation for their children, so that they always came out top of the educational system; would we then think that poorer children did not have equality of opportunity, because they had no opportunity to get rid of their genetic disadvantages?

Here we might think that our notion of personal identity itself was beginning to give way; we might well wonder *who were* the people whose advantages and disadvantages were being discussed in this way. But it would be wrong, I think, to try to solve this problem simply by saying that in the supposed circumstances our notion of personal identity would have collapsed in such a way that we could no longer speak of the individuals involved—in the end, we could still pick out the individuals by spatio-temporal criteria, if no more. Our objections against the system suggested in this fantasy must, I think, be moral rather than metaphysical. They need not concern us here. What is interesting about the fantasy, perhaps, is that if one reached this state of affairs, the individuals would be regarded as in all respects equal in themselves—for in themselves they would be, as it were, pure subjects or bearers

[4] A yet more radical situation—but one more likely to come about—would be that in which an individual's characteristics could be *pre-arranged* by interference with the genetic material. The dizzying consequences of this I shall not try to explore.

of predicates, everything else about them, including their genetic inheritance, being regarded as a fortuitous and changeable characteristic. In these circumstances, where everything about a person is controllable, equality of opportunity and absolute equality seem to coincide; and this itself illustrates something about the notion of equality of opportunity.

I said that we need not discuss here the moral objections to the kind of world suggested in this fantasy. There is, however, one such point that is relevant to the different aspects of equality that have been discussed in this paper as a whole. One objection that we should instinctively feel about the fantasy world is that far too much emphasis was being placed on achieving high ability; that the children were just being regarded as locations of abilities. I think we should still feel this even if everybody (with results hard to imagine) was treated in this way; when not everybody was so treated, the able would also be more successful than others, and those very concerned with producing the ability would probably also be over-concerned with success. The moral objections to the excessive concern with such aims are, interestingly, not unconnected with the ideal of equality itself; they are connected with equality in the sense discussed in the earlier sections of this paper, the equality of human beings despite their differences, and in particular with the complex of notions considered in the second section under the heading of "respect."

This conflict within the ideals of equality arises even without resort to the fantasy world. It exists to-day in the feeling that a thorough-going emphasis on equality of opportunity must destroy a certain sense of common humanity which is itself an ideal of equality.[5] The ideals that are felt to be in conflict with equality of opportunity are not necessarily other ideals of equality—there may be an independent appeal to the values of community life, or to the moral worth of a more integrated and less competitive society. Nevertheless, the idea of equality itself is often invoked in this connexion, and not, I think, inappropriately.

If the idea of equality ranges as widely as I have suggested, this type of conflict is bound to arise with it. It is an idea which, on the one hand, is invoked in connexion with the distribution

[5] See, for example, Michael Young, *The Rise of the Meritocracy,* London: Thames and Hudson, 1958.

of certain goods, some at least of which are bound to confer on their possessors some preferred status or prestige. On the other hand, the idea of equality of respect is one which urges us to give less consideration to those structures in which people enjoy status or prestige, and to consider people independently of those goods, on the distribution of which equality of opportunity precisely focuses our, and their, attention. There is perhaps nothing formally incompatible in these two applications of the idea of equality: one might hope for a society in which there existed both a fair, rational and appropriate distribution of these goods, and no contempt, condescension or lack of human communication between persons who were more and less successful recipients of the distribution. Yet in actual fact, there are deep psychological and social obstacles to the realization of this hope; as things are, the competitiveness and considerations of prestige that surround the first application of equality certainly militate against the second. How far this situation is inevitable, and how far in an economically developed and dynamic society, in which certain skills and talents are necessarily at a premium, the obstacles to a wider realization of equality might be overcome, I do not think that we know: these are in good part questions of psychology and sociology, to which we do not have the answers.

When one is faced with the spectacle of the various elements of the idea of equality pulling in these different directions, there is a strong temptation, if one does not abandon the idea altogether, to abandon some of its elements: to claim, for instance, that equality of opportunity is the only ideal that is at all practicable, and equality of respect a vague and perhaps nostalgic illusion; or, alternatively, that equality of respect is genuine equality, and equality of opportunity an inegalitarian betrayal of the ideal—all the more so if it were thoroughly pursued, as now it is not. To succumb to either of these simplifying formulæ would, I think, be a mistake. Certainly, a highly rational and efficient application of the ideas of equal opportunity, unmitigated by the other considerations, could lead to a quite inhuman society (if it worked—which, granted a well-known desire of parents to secure a position for their children at least as good as their own, is unlikely). On the other hand, an ideal of equality of respect that made no contact with such things as the economic needs of society for certain skills, and human desire for some sorts of prestige, would be condemned to a futile Utopianism, and to having no rational effect on the distribution of goods, position and power that would inevitably proceed. If, moreover, as I have suggested, it is not really known how far, by new forms of social structure and of education, these conflicting claims might be reconciled, it is all the more obvious that we should not throw one set of claims out of the window; but should rather seek, in each situation, the best way of eating and having as much cake as possible. It is an uncomfortable situation, but the discomfort is just that of genuine political thought. It is no greater with equality than it is with liberty, or any other noble and substantial political ideal.

J. R. LUCAS

Against Equality

Equality is the great political issue of our time. Liberty is forgotten: Fraternity never did engage our passions: the maintenance of Law and Order is at a discount: Natural Rights and Natural Justice are outmoded shibboleths. But Equality—there men have something to die for, kill for, agitate about, be miserable about. The demand for Equality obsesses all our political thought. We are not sure what it is—indeed, as I shall show later, we are necessarily not sure what it is—but we are sure that whatever it is, we want it: and while we are prepared to look on frustration, injustice or violence with tolerance, as part of the natural order of things, we will work ourselves up into paroxysms of righteous indignation at the bare mention of Inequality.

For my own part, I think the current obsession with Equality deplorable. There are problems enough in all conscience, to occupy our minds for the rest of this century, without inculcating in each man's breast a feeling of resentment because in some respect or other he compares unfavourably with somebody else. But it is not enough to deplore; and my attack will take the more insidious form of understanding Equality. I shall show why it is that we are tempted to demand Equality, and in what sense the demand is rational; and how we have been confused into thinking that our demand is for something else; and how this demand is incoherent,

J. R. Lucas, "Against Equality," *Philosophy,* XL (October 1965), pp. 296–307. Reprinted by permission of the author and The Royal Institute of Philosophy.

because what is demanded is both internally inconsistent and incompatible with other more precious ideals.

We are tempted to demand Equality when we set out to give a moral or rational critique of society. Not that it is wrong to try to give a rational account of one's society, although one should not be too doctrinaire about it; the crude realist, who is concerned only with what he can get away with, is not an estimable creature. And although the historical approach is estimable, and adequate for explaining why things are as they are, yet since the future can never be exactly like the past, it gives us only inadequate guidance on how political choices are to be made. To this extent at least, we ought to attempt a moral and rational critique of our society. Of those who have done so, most have laid it down either that men are all equal really, or that they ought to be. This Equality, which is a by-product of rationality, is nothing other than the principle of Universalisability. I shall call it the principle of Formal Equality. It requires that if two people are being treated, or are to be treated, differently, there should be some relevant difference between them. Otherwise, in the absence of some differentiating feature, what is sauce for the goose is sauce for the gander, and it would be wrong to treat the two unequally, that is, not the same.

It is clear that Formal Equality by itself establishes very little. Indeed, if we accept the infinite variety of human personality, that no two people, not even identical twins, are qualitatively identical, then there will always be differences between any two people, which might be held to justify a difference of treatment. Many of these differences we may wish to rule out as not being relevant, but since the principle of Formal Equality does not provide, of itself, any criteria of relevance, it does not, by itself, establish much. It gives a line of argument, but not any definite conclusion.

Egalitarians, however, profess to be less concerned with differences than with samenesses. The ways in which men resemble one another are much more important, they hold, than the ways in which they differ, and a corresponding similarity of treatment is the only one that can be justified. It seems at first sight to be a natural corollary—a contraposition almost—of the principle of Formal Equality. The latter states that people may properly be treated differently only if they are different: the former that since people are, in fact, similar, their treatment should be similar too. A moment's reflection, however, will show that the equivalence is spurious. It is spurious because the respects in which people are, in the one case the same, in the other different, are not themselves the same. Human beings are the same in respect of being featherless bipeds, of being sentient agents, perhaps rational ones, perhaps children of God. They are not the same in respect of height, age, sex, intellectual ability, strength of character. These latter differences may be irrelevant, as the egalitarians assert: but they are not proved not to be differences by the fact that in other respects men are similar.

The argument from sameness is thus seen to be independent of the principle of Formal Equality. It is often expressed by the words "After all, all men are men" or "A man is a man for a' that." It would be difficult to deny what is stated in these words, but difficult also to derive very convincingly from it any principle of Equality. The argument, inasmuch as there is one, seems to run thus:

All men are men
All men are equally men
∴ All men are equal.

It is not, on the face of it, a cogent form of argument. That it is in fact fallacious is shown by the parody which can be obtained by replacing the word "men" by the word "numbers."

All numbers are numbers
All numbers are equally numbers
∴ All numbers are equal.

An implicit and illegitimate extension is being made of the respects in virtue of which the men (or numbers) are being said to be equal; it has been assumed that because they are equal in some respects—in possessing those characteristics in virtue of which they are said to be men—therefore they are equal in all. And this does not follow.

Nevertheless, we do think that *something* follows from the fact that men are men, and that all men share a common humanity. We do think that men, because they are men, ought not to be killed, tortured, imprisoned, exploited, frustrated, humiliated; that they should never be treated merely as means but always also as ends in themselves. Exactly what is meant is unclear, but at least two things are clear: that all men are entitled to such treatment; and that their entitlement derives from their possession of certain features, such as sentience and rationality, which are characteristic of the human species. And therefore it is proper to view the argument as one which starts from the universal common humanity of men—that all men are men—and ends with an injunction about how men are to be treated—that all men are to be treated alike, *in certain respects.* Although thus set out, the argument would not find favour with tough-minded philosophers, it is a sound argument so far as it goes. Only, it has little to do with Equality. It is, rather, an argument of Universal Humanity, that we should treat human beings, because they are human beings, humanely. To say that all men, because they are men, are equally men, or that to treat any two persons as ends in themselves is to treat them as equally ends in themselves is to import a spurious note of egalitarianism into a perfectly sound and serious argument. We may call it, if we like, the argument from Equality of Respect, but in this phrase it is the word "Respect"—respect for each man's humanity, respect for him as a human being—which is doing the logical work, while the word "Equality" adds nothing to the argument and is altogether otiose.

The principle of Formal Equality or Universalisability, and the principle of Equality of Respect, or Universal Humanity, are two extremes, bounding the range in which seriously egalitarian principles of Equality operate. We have two universes of discourse to correlate: one consists of human beings, the other of possible treatments of human beings. Each human being is characterised by an infinite (or at least indefinitely large) number of characteristics, and we correlate (or "map") the universe of possible treatments with the universe of human beings thus characterised. One principle, the principle of Universalisability, expresses for one type of correlation the fact that it is one-valued; that is, that every distinction which can be drawn between treatments corresponds to some distinction which can be drawn between human beings; but this is always possible since no two people are qualitatively identical: the other principle, that of Universal Humanity, expresses for another type of correlation the fact that it correlates characteristics common to all human beings with characteristics common to all humane treatments. The principle of Universalisability specifies the treatment as fully as any one, egalitarian or non-egalitarian, could want, but in doing this for the treatments, is committed to drawing too many distinctions among the human beings for the egalitarian to stomach. The principle of Universal Humanity manages not to distinguish between men, so as to gladden the heart of the egalitarian: but in saying so little about men as not to differentiate between them, it says too little about treatments to characterise them in more than a very minimal way—too little to ensure that they all will be equal in the way that the egalitarian wants. The egalitarian wants a map of the logical possibilities which is very detailed—in order to have everybody treated alike *in all respects*—and at the same time a crude outline sketch—in order to include all men together in only one constituency: but the logical manoeuvres which will give him the one will preclude him from having the other, and *vice versa*. More than logical considerations will be required to lead us from the minimal specification of human beings, which is the only one in respect of which we are all alike, to the maximal specification of the treatments we are to receive, which is necessary if they are all to be thought to be the same.

The central argument for Equality is a muddle. There are two sound principles of political reasoning, the principle of Universalisability and the principle of Universal Humanity, and each has been described as a sort of Equality, Formal Equality in the one case and Equality of Respect in the other. But they are not the same Equality, nor are they compatible, and they cannot be run in harness to lead to a full-blooded egalitarianism. Each, however, by itself can lead to some conclusions which an egalitarian would endorse. Though these conclusions are less, and necessarily less, than all that an egalitarian would wish, they represent the only Equalities that are obtainable and are reasonable to seek.

The principle of Universalisability is not vacuous in political reasoning because a polity is governed by laws, and laws involve universal terms. Laws are couched in universal terms partly for practical reasons, though not for them alone. There is not time to take into account all the characteristics of each person or all the features of each case: we cannot give separate orders to 50 million people individually, but have to make relatively few and blunt discriminations, lumping people together in categories and applying general rules to them, laying down what *motorists* are required to do, what *householders* are entitled to do, what *customers'* rights are. Exceptions[1] must be rare: for the most part laws must be no respectors of persons.

[1] E.g. in a monarchy, the monarch: Elizabeth II has no private existence and

Practical considerations apart, there are two other reasons for laws being couched in universal terms.[2] The first is that laws ought to be just: not absolutely just—we realise that absolute justice, like any other absolute ideal, is unattainable in this imperfect world—but guided by a certain aspiration towards justice. It is—and here I part company with many modern writers on jurisprudence—essential to our notion of law and our being willing to obey it, that it should be administered by courts which are courts of *justice*, and determined by judges having as their ideal the blind goddess who holds the scales and is no respector of persons but gives her decision in accordance with the merits of the case. But if the decisions of the court are to have any semblance of justice, they must be based on certain general features of the case, held to be relevant; and therefore laws themselves ought to be couched in universal terms, so that the justice dispensed in accordance with them shall conform at least to this necessary condition of being just.

The second reason for couching laws in general terms is to protect the subject from the government, and to enable him to know what the law requires of him so that he may be free to plan his life accordingly. It is an argument from imperfection: imperfection of the governors, imperfection of the governed. We want to make sure that our governors, our rulers, our judges cannot abuse their authority, or subject any one man to covert pressure to conform to their wishes: and we know that many men are not motivated altogether by ideals of absolute morality, and may want to do things which another man might regard as wrong, and that therefore they need to know in advance where they stand, and what things they may, and what things they may not, do. And so we require that laws shall be published beforehand, and apply to people generally, and not pick out any one person rather than another except in so far as he falls under some universal description.

Formal Equality thus becomes, in political reasoning, something much more substantial, namely Equality before the Law; but the Equality it establishes is still not an egalitarian Equality. Justice has her eyes blindfolded: only those considerations which go into the scales are weighed. That is to say, not every factor is

---

is quite unlike anybody else. Our laws are not couched altogether in universal terms, and do pay peculiar respect to the person of the Monarch.

[2] For a much fuller account, see Morris Ginsberg, "The Concept of Justice," *Philosophy* (1963), pp. 99–116.

relevant. Thus Equality before the Law will secure men equal treatment in some respects at the cost of necessarily not securing men equal treatment in all respects: the guilty are not treated the same as the innocent; the rich are often, and rightly, not fined the same as the poor; the mere fact of conviction may ruin a schoolmaster or a civil servant while constituting only a small penalty to a man of independent means. Equality before the Law is nonetheless valuable for that. It secures to all the protection of the law—no man is to be outside the law, and everyone shall have access to the courts to vindicate his rights against every other man. It secures the uniform administration of the law without fear or favour. It gives the subject protection against arbitrary decisions by those in authority, and it gives him freedom to make rational plans. These are reasons enough to value Equality before the Law and on occasion to enact further measures—the provision of Legal Aid, for example—the better to secure it. But the Equality vouchsafed us by Equality before the Law, although valuable and not vacuous, is still much less than the Equality the egalitarian seeks.

Equality before the Law does not of itself secure that the laws themselves are equal. In one sense, they cannot be. Laws must pick out particular classes of people, actions, situations. The Traffic Acts apply, for instance, mainly to motorists, not to motorists and nonmotorists alike. Nevertheless, we can criticise certain laws, not for discriminating, but for discriminating irrelevantly. It is irrelevant to a man's right to own property or to travel in buses that his skin is of a certain colour, though not, presumably, to his being employed as an actor in the part of Iago. It is irrelevant to whether a man should be allowed to exceed the speed limit that he is rich or that he is not rich, though not that he is a policeman in pursuit of a criminal, and arguably not that he is a doctor going to the scene of an accident. Many of the discriminations the egalitarian objects to, we can object to too, but because they offend against the canons of rationality and justice. Laws ought to be, so far as possible, rational and just, and therefore the distinctions drawn by each law should be relevant ones with regard to the general purpose of the law. But—and here is the rub—there is no sharp criterion of relevance, and sometimes, indeed, the mere fact that some people think something is relevant is enough to make it so. Many of the most serious disputes of our age are really disputes about relevance. The superficial slogans of the egalitarian are no help. If we want to have fruitful discussions about political matters, we must replace controversies about Equality by detailed arguments about *criteria* of *relevance.*[3] Being arguments, they are naturally two-sided, and one side may be right without the other being unreasonable, and an opponent may be wrong without being necessarily wrong-headed. In the detailed assessment of argument we shall see the important truth which the idiom of egalitarianism conceals, that on most political questions we are presented with a balance of argument rather than a simple black-and-white issue. Our arguments, therefore, will yield conclusions that are more solidly based, yet more tolerant in tone. Some, but not all, the conclusions the egalitarian yearns for can be maintained on nonegalitarian grounds, better established, but less censoriously affirmed.

In a similar vein the argument from Equality of Respect, Universal Humanity, will produce some of the conclusions the egalitarian looks for, but not the essentially egalitarian ones. Whenever inequality results in some people having *too little,* the humanitarian will protest as well as the egalitarian. Human life cannot be properly lived in very straitened circumstances, and we do not show respect for human beings as such if we do not try to alleviate those conditions. Moreover, wealth and poverty are, in part, relative terms: it is not just that there is a certain minimum requirement of food and fuel—true though this is: there is also a varying, and in our age rising, level of normality in each particular community, and to be too far below this will preclude a man from participation in the normal life of that community. The pre-war poor scholars in Oxford did not usually suffer from undernourishment: but their poverty did prevent them living the

[3] Or, to be exact, both criteria of *relevance* and criteria of *irrelevance.* Sometimes the onus of proof is on the man who claims that a certain factor is relevant, sometimes on him who denies it. Differences of skin-pigmentation may be presumed irrelevant, unless the contrary is shown, on any question of employment: differences of hair-pigmentation may be presumed relevant, unless the contrary is shown, in a beauty contest. Very roughly, in public life there is a presumption of irrelevance, and we will not be happy about any distinction in the Law, in public service, in the conditions of public employment, or in the award of public contracts unless it can be shown to be relevant: whereas in private life there is a presumption of relevance, and we are disposed to accept any distinction a private individual draws, unless it is clearly an irrelevant one.

normal life of an undergraduate, and could be objected to on those grounds alone. Not only bread, but Nescafé and books are necessaries of university life—of social existence rather than bare physical subsistence.

This argument, the argument of the rising minimum as I shall call it, is by far the most pervasive argument in political thought today. It is a telling argument, but it is open to abuse. It may be a good thing that nobody should be without a television set: but it is only one *desideratum* among many; it does not have, though sometimes pretends to have, the compelling force of the claim that nobody should be without food.

The argument of the rising minimum ought not only to be tentative in its forcefulness, but moderate in its claims, and ought not to set its sights too high. We may say that people ought not to fall too far below the average: we must be careful not to be led into saying that people must not fall at all below the average. The latter would entail a strict Equality: but it cannot be justified on any argument from humanity, however much extended. For there are differences too small to make any substantial difference —for example, if I can afford to invite only thirty-nine people to a party, whereas the average is forty. If negligible differences are to matter, it must be because comparisons are being made, not because their consequences are important. People are feeling put upon *not* because they cannot join in normal activities, but because they *mind* that they have got less than other people. But then the argument has ceased to be an argument from humanity plus, and has become an argument from envy, an argument strong no doubt in many breasts, but a different one, nonetheless, and of a different degree of cogency.

The argument from extended humanity cannot set the minimum acceptable level too close to the average. It therefore cannot require that there should not be any people getting more than the average, and in particular, that there should not be some people getting much more than the average. This is the acid test for distinguishing the true egalitarian from the humanitarian. The true egalitarian will object on principle to any one man having much more than any others, even if, by reducing the one man's possessions, the others would attain only a negligible benefit, or none at all. The humanitarian has no such objection in principle. He may on occasion play Robin Hood, but only if he is convinced that the beneficiaries are in real need and will be substantially benefited by redistribution and that the arguments against intervening are less weighty than the arguments for. Equality of Respect will produce some but not all the conclusions the egalitarian desires, not the peculiarly egalitarian ones.

Having gone thus far in pursuit of Equality, we have gone as far as we can reasonably go. Legality, Justice, Fairness, Equity, Humanity, all will on occasion produce a measure of Equality, but the measure is never exact, and they are none of them essentially egalitarian. The Equality that goes further than this, the Equality that the egalitarian yearns for, is unattainable and, to my mind, undesirable. It may be partly a matter of taste; I like variety more than I like uniformity: but it is also an inescapable conclusion from the nature of society and a consideration of the *desiderata* we have for a society's being a good one.[4] If men, as we now know them, are to co-exist in civil society there must be sanctions: this follows from the fact that some people are bloody-minded, and will do violence to others unless restrained by force or the threat of force. Civil society is, therefore, dependent on there being a system of coercion, and hence on there being certain people in a position to coerce others, people, that is, with power. Power cannot be equally divided and distributed over the whole population. It is necessarily concentrated in few hands. Egalitarians may take steps to make the possession of power in some sense more equal, but even in so doing they admit its natural inequality. Power is concentrated in some hands rather than others, and since power is one of the goods that men desire, it follows that in any society in which there are, or may be, bloody-minded men, there must be some people who possess more of the good that is constituted by power than do others.

Besides an inequality of power, there is an inequality of prestige, which will arise in any society which is in Durkheim's phrase "a moral community"—whose members, that is, share values and have some ideals in common. It will stem from men's natural inequality of ability resulting in their being able, some to a greater, others to a lesser, extent to be successful in achieving their ideals. There will thus be an inequality of success, and therefore also of prestige,

[4] See, for example, Ralf Dahrendorf, "On the Origin of Social Inequality," in *Philosophy Politics and Society*, ed. Peter Laslett and W. G. Runciman, pp. 88–109.

which has nothing to do with power or sanctions. There are many sanctionless sub-societies which form moral communities and are correspondingly stratified. Undergraduates provide one example. There are no sanctions, no undergraduates "in power," but some undergraduates do succeed more than others in realising some undergraduate ideal of excellence. The President of the Union, of O.U.D.S., of the J.C.R., are each top of his own particular tree and have more prestige than the rest of us. Again, in the world of science or in the republic of letters, there is no parity of esteem between all members. In these societies the members are not even located in one place, so there is no possibility of force being used or coercion required. Nevertheless there is a loosely established hierarchy, with all its inevitable inequalities. Shared ideals and inequality of ability is thus enough to bring about this sort of inequality, inequality of prestige. Whereas even if all men were of equal ability, or had no community of ideals, we should still, provided only that they lived in the same place and some of them might be tempted to use force, have an inequality of power.

It follows, then, that we shall never be able to avoid some inequalities; we can never avoid some inequality of power and we cannot avoid an inequality of prestige, unless we are prepared to have our society not be a moral community, but only a minimal civil society—and one of the lessons we can draw from political history since the time of John Locke is that most people will not be content with so bare a form of coexistence. They look to society not merely for security but for the opportunity of realising themselves in social existence, and are always creating the conditions for inequality of prestige.

Since men value power and prestige as much as the possession of wealth—indeed, these three "goods" cannot be completely separated—it is foolish to seek to establish an equality of wealth on egalitarian grounds. It is foolish first because it will not result in what egalitarians really want. It is foolish also because if we do not let men compete for money, they will compete all the more for power; and whereas the possession of wealth by another man does not hurt me, unless I am made vulnerable by envy, the possession of power by another is inherently dangerous; and furthermore if we are to maintain a strict equality of wealth we need a much greater apparatus of state to secure it and therefore a much greater inequality of power. Better have bloated plutocrats than omnipotent bureaucrats.

It might be tempting to deal with power the way the Athenians did—accept that it must be of its nature unequal, but distribute it by lot. If we cannot all have an equal share of power, at least we can all have an equal chance of it. It is noteworthy that this is the method adopted by our egalitarian age of distributing another essentially unequal good in an egalitarian fashion. Great wealth is obviously inegalitarian; but nonetheless coveted for that. The pools create fortunes at negligible cost to their "investors," and distribute them at random. The unintelligent and unindustrious have just as much a chance as the energetic and the thrifty. This is their attraction—there is no damned merit about them. And so we do not tax winnings in the way we tax earnings. Our objection to non-random assignments of wealth is the same as the Athenians' objection to elective office: some people are more likely to get rich or get elected than others, and the others know it, and do not like it. Justice is not blind enough: only Ernie is truly no respector of persons.

But there is a snag. Just as we pay a heavy price for preferring Equality to efficiency, and assigning economic rewards on the impartial basis of chance rather than any criteria of effort or enterprise, so the Athenians found the lot producing ineffectual rulers. And power must follow ability. So the *strategoi,* who were elected and could be chosen for their merits, came to exercise power, not the Archons, selected as they were by lot from a large field. The lesson holds good for us. We demand too much of government, we depend too much on its being tolerably competent, for us to be able to sacrifice all considerations of efficiency upon the altar of Equality. We can, and should, take special measures to prevent the abuse of power; but we cannot confine that essentially unequal concept in an egalitarian mould, and if we attempt to do so, we shall find that power has fled from our equalled hands, and has taken on some new, and much less controllable, form.

Even where we can secure Equality, it is often not desirable. The administration of justice is better served by selecting good judges and putting them in a highly unequal position *vis-à-vis* the litigants, than by having a large number of equally eligible *dikastai,* who have no powers to secure the fair conduct of the case. Better laws are likely to be enacted if legislators are unequally privileged in the matter of free speech, and can say in Parliament all sorts of things which would be actionable elsewhere. The choice between economic efficiency and economic Equality is one we are all familiar with, and one that is likely to become more and more pressing in the next decade. If we are to attach any weight to merit—and it is difficult to claim that fairness is preserved where merit is disregarded—we are committed to possible inequalities of some sort, because although it cannot be shown *a priori* that people do have different deserts, it does follow from the nature of the concept that they could. In the same way, Equality of opportunity, whatever the other difficulties of that dubious concept, clearly precludes the certainty of Equality of achievement. If, as is sometimes demanded by politicians, everybody ought to have an equal chance of getting into Oxford, it still means (unless the chance is either unity or zero) that some people will, and others will not, get in. The 18-plus is going the same way as the 11-plus, and from having been the ark of the egalitarian covenant is becoming the symbol of inegalitarian wickedness. This change of front reflects neither dishonesty nor outstanding stupidity on the part of egalitarians, but the internal inconsistency of their ideal, absolute Equality. We can secure Equality in certain respects between members of certain classes for certain purposes and under certain conditions; but never, and necessarily never, Equality in all respects between all men for all purposes and under all conditions. The egalitarian is doomed to a life not only of grumbling and everlasting envy, but of endless and inevitable disappointment.

These, perhaps, are arguments which appeal more to conservatives than radicals. Let me end therefore by pointing out the incompatibility of Equality with the other two traditional ideals of radicalism, Fraternity and Liberty.

Fraternity does in part involve one of our concepts of Equality, Equality of Respect, Universal Humanity. But it demands the negation of other Equalities, Formal Equality and the various egalitarian Equalities. It demands that we treat each person as a person for him-, or her-, self and not simply as the bearer of certain characteristics; the demand is that I should "love you for yourself alone, and not your yellow hair." Whatever the logical difficulties in this, at least it amounts to a protest against the paper world in which people are treated not as people but as beings conforming to specifications. We regard ourselves as individuals, each one different, each one a whole person, knobbly, not fitting exactly into any mould: and we do not like it if, in the name of Equality or anything else, we are wrapped up and put in a carton and labelled, indistinguishably from a lot of others. We want to be ourselves, and to be able to get through to other people, rough uncut diamonds though they may be, not separated from them by layers of tissue paper establishing a flabby uniformity between us all. Inevitably in a large society the demand for Fraternity cannot be pushed very far. Personal relationships are emotionally absorbing and time-consuming; we cannot have them with many people. With most people our relationship must be to some extent official, to some extent formal, based on incomplete knowledge and incomplete attention, and therefore determined by only some of the characteristics of the person concerned, not by them all. We cannot be fully fraternal with the public. But we can resist the attempt to make all our private arrangements subject to the formalities that properly pertain only to public ones, and we can resist public encroachment on private affairs; and in so far as we do, we shall be denying the Equalities that egalitarians strive for.

Liberty imposes like limitations. Only, whereas Fraternity limits Equality at the receiving end—the person dealt with wants to be considered as himself, not as the possessor of certain characteristics—, Liberty limits Equality at the doing end—the person who is doing the dealing wants to be free to make his own choices, and not required always to treat similar cases similarly. Equality lays down how we are to treat people: but Liberty entitles us to act as we choose, not as some rule lays down. If I have any Liberty then there are some decisions I am allowed to make on my own; I am free in some cases to act arbitrarily. And if that is so, I may in such cases arbitrarily choose one person rather than another, without there being any ground to justify discrimination. I may choose Jane, and take her to wife, while passing over Bess, her equally well-favoured sister. This is what it is to be free. Freedom is inherently unfair. If we place any value on Freedom at all, we must to that extent compromise the principle of Equality. And we must place some value on Freedom, for to be free in some respects is a necessary condition of discovering oneself as a moral and rational agent. And only for such can the question of Equality arise.

STANLEY I. BENN

Egalitarianism and the Equal Consideration of Interests

Egalitarians persist in speaking of human equality, as a principle significant for action, in the face of all the evident human inequalities of stature, physique, intellect, virtue, merit, and desert. Claims pressed so tenaciously, in the face of seemingly manifest and overwhelming objections, can hardly be summarily dismissed as naive absurdities. The task for the philosopher is to look for ways of construing such claims, consistent with the evident inequalities, compatible with commonly accepted conceptions of justice, yet still with bite enough to make a difference to behavior worth contending for. I shall argue that in many contexts the claim to human equality is no more than a negative egalitarianism, a denial, a limited criticism of some specific existing arrangements. If one were to interpret such claims as implying a universal positive assertion about human rights and social organization, one would be going beyond what was necessary to make good sense of them. But because such a negative interpretation does not seem to exhaust the possibilities of egalitarianism, I shall formulate a principle that, while satisfying the aforementioned criteria, can still be applied quite generally, and can be properly expressed in the formula "all men are equal." This is the *principle of equal consideration of human interests*. I shall further maintain that this

Stanley I. Benn, "Egalitarianism and the Equal Consideration of Interests," in J. Roland Pennock and John W. Chapman, eds., *Nomos IX: Equality*, pp. 61–78. Reprinted by permission of the publishers, Atherton Press, Inc.

principle is required by current conceptions of social justice. It can be effective in public policy-making, however, only to the extent that agreement can be reached on the proper order of priority of human interests.

Things or persons can be equal in several different ways. In one sense equality presupposes an ordering of objects according to some common natural property or attribute that can be possessed in varying degrees. So, although objects said to be equal occupy interchangeable places in such an ordering, their equality in this respect is necessarily implied neither by their possessing this property in common nor by their common membership of a larger class of which all members possess the property. Although two cabbages happen, for instance, to be of equal weight, their equality is not a necessary feature of their both being cabbages, even though every cabbage has weight. In this sense at least, not all cabbages are equal. Things can be equal in a second sense according to some standard of value or merit. Two students' essays may be equally good, though their properties may differ, one being detailed and painstaking, the other original and imaginative. Here, differences in their properties are weighed against one another in assessing their relative merit; however, in a final ordering of all essays, in which some stand high and others low, these two occupy interchangeable places. Here, again, their equality is not a necessary feature of their both being essays. A third kind of equality is that of need, entitlement, or desert; the remuneration to which a man is entitled for his work or the dose of medicine he needs for his cough may be equal to another's, though it could conceivably have been different without prejudice to their common status as workers or sick men.

These three ways of ascribing equality—descriptive, evaluative, and distributive—are not of course independent of one another. There may be a logical connection: two knives, equally sharp, equally well-tempered, possessing indeed all relevant properties in the same degree, are equally good knives, sharpness, temper, and the like, being the criteria of a good knife.[1] However, the equal merit of the students' essays does not follow necessarily from

[1] The phrase "possessing all relevant properties to the same degree" guarantees the tautology, of course, by exhausting all the possible criteria.

a list of their properties but depends on a complex appraisal in the light of multiple standards. Different again is the case of two men entitled to equal pay for doing equal amounts of work. In this case, their equality depends on a particular convention; according to a different practice, if one man worked longer than the other, their deserts would be different, even though the results might be the same. In all these instances, however, though the possibility of comparison depends on the subjects being members of the same class, it is not a necessary condition of their membership that they possess the property by virtue of which they are equals in the precise degree that they do. Mere membership of the same class does not entail, therefore, that the subjects are equals in any of the three senses discussed. Consequently, although two members of a class happen to qualify for equal treatment, this is not a necessary result of their common membership.

To say, then, that two things are in some respect equal is to say that they are, in that and perhaps related respects, interchangeable—that no rational ground exists for treating them in those respects differently from each other. Egalitarians would maintain, however, that the reason for considering them equal need not always be that they satisfy some qualifying condition to the same degree; it may be because, with regard to some manner of treating them, the qualifying condition does not admit of degrees; it may be enough simply to possess the properties necessary to make them members of that class. There may then be something to which all members of a class have an equal claim, in the sense that none has a better claim than another, nor could have, given their common membership. If, for instance, all sane adults have the right to vote, and there are no other qualifying (or disqualifying) conditions, no qualified member of the class of sane adults has any better right than another, nor has any member a right to any more votes than another, by virtue of some further property that they possesss in varying degrees. All qualified voters, qua voters, are equal.

Those who demand social equality do not necessarily take universal adult equal suffrage as a paradigm for all social institutions and practices. There may be egalitarians for whom a society without differences is both a possibility and an ideal; most, however, have more limited aims. When egalitarianism is translated into concrete political programs, it usually amounts to a proposal to abandon existing inequalities, rather than to adopt some positive principle of social justice. The egalitarian in politics usually has quite specific objectives and is critical of quite specific kinds of differentiation rather than of every kind of social discrimination. Indeed, differences are rarely called "inequalities" unless, in the first place, they affect the things which men value and for which they compete, like power, wealth, or esteem. One complains of inequality if one has to pay more tax than another man but not if, for some administrative reason, the demands arrive in differently colored envelopes. Egalitarians protest when, in the second place, they see no rational justification for differentiating a particular class for the purpose of allocating certain specific privileges or burdens. The campaign for equal pay for women is a case in point. To treat people according to their skill or productivity would not be to discriminate between the sexes, even though some women might in fact receive less than some men (or, conceivably, all women less than all men), for skill and productivity are generally recognized as relevant and legitimate criteria. Sex differentiation as such is intolerable because, it is argued, no one has yet shown good enough reasons for thinking a person's sex relevant to the income he should earn—and the burden of proof rests on the discriminator. On the other hand, discrimination according to sex for military service has been generally accepted without much question and is usually considered well-grounded; so it is rarely called an inequality.

A race, sex, religious, or class egalitarianism denies the justice, then, of some existing modes of discrimination, possibly in a relatively limited range of social practices; it does not press for the removal of all forms of differentiation. Or it may endorse existing grounds of discrimination but question whether they ought to make as much difference as they do. Of course, the conditions under attack, and the related forms of differentiation not under attack, may be contextually supplied and not explicitly stated; nevertheless, they may be perfectly well understood by all parties to the debate.[2]

[2] A favorite way of discrediting the egalitarian, however, is to make it appear that he seeks to remove forms of discrimination that neither he, nor anyone else, would for a moment question. Though the Levellers were concerned only for equal political rights, for removing monopolistic privileges in trade, and for legal reforms, they were frequently accused, despite vigorous disclaimers, of wanting to level property.

Although most movements for equality can be interpreted in terms of protests against specific inequalities, a strong disposition nonetheless exists, among philosophers and others, to argue that whatever men's actual differences and whatever their genuine relevance for certain kinds of differentiation, there yet remain important values in respect of which all men's claims are equal. Whatever these may be—and catalogs of natural and human rights are attempts to formulate them—they are such that no difference in properties between one man and another could affect them; all men qualify simply by virtue of belonging to the class *man*, which admits of no degrees (just as, in my earlier examples, all voters are equally qualified provided they are sane adults). This certainly looks like a positive and quite general claim to equality rather than a denial of specific irrelevant inequalities.

In a recent article, "Against Equality,"[3] J. R. Lucas contends that egalitarianism rests on a confusion of two principles, each sound in itself but which, if pressed, together lead to incompatible conclusions. One, the principle of formal equality, is the familiar principle underlying all forms of what I have called negative egalitarianism: if two people are to be treated differently there should be some relevant difference between them. Lucas does not regard this as really an egalitarian principle at all, because in itself it prescribes neither equality nor inequality, but, taking it for granted that there might be good reasons for treating men differently in some respects, it lays down the form that a justificatory argument must take. The other principle, that Lucas calls the principle of universal humanity, makes this assertion:

> men, because they are men, ought not to be killed, tortured, imprisoned, exploited, frustrated, humiliated; . . . they should never be treated merely as means but always as ends in themselves. . . . We should treat human beings, because they are human beings, humanely.

But this, he says, has little to do with equality:

> To say that all men, because they are men, are equally men, or that to treat any two persons as ends in themselves is to treat them as equally ends in themselves is to import a spurious note of egalitarianism into a perfectly sound and serious argument. We may

[3] *Philosophy*, XL (1965), pp. 296–307. [Pp. 138–151 above.]—ED.

> call it, if we like, the argument for Equality of Respect, but in this phrase it is the word "Respect"—respect for each man's humanity, respect for him as a human being—which is doing the logical work, while the word "Equality" adds nothing to the argument and is altogether otiose.[4]

I suspect that Lucas has dealt too shortly with positive egalitarianism, in representing it simply as rules about how we ought to behave in relation to objects or persons of a given class. He is perfectly right in saying, for instance, that the duty not to inflict torture has nothing to do with equality, but then, it is not a duty in respect of human beings alone but also of animals. This is not a duty we *owe* to men as men, for it is doubtful whether, properly speaking, we *owe* it to the object at all. Inflicting needless pain is simply wrong; it would not be a case of unequal treatment, but simply of cruelty. It would be a case lacking altogether the characteristic feature that makes inequality objectionable—namely, unfairness or injustice.

But some of Lucas' examples of inhumanity do seem to have more to do with equality than that. In particular, the injunction to respect all men, simply as men or as ends in themselves, unlike the injunction not to torture them, involves recognizing them as subjects of claims, and not merely as objects, albeit objects that ought to be handled in one way rather than another. To treat a man not as an end but simply as a means is to give no consideration to his interests, but to consider him only insofar as he can promote or frustrate the interests of someone else—to treat him, in sort, like Aristotle's "natural slave," with no end not derived from that of a master. Now to adopt such an attitude can be said to be not merely wrong (as is cruelty), but wrong in the special way that it disregards a fundamental equality of *claim*—the claim to have one's interests considered alongside those of everyone else likely to be affected by the decision.

Now this *principle of equal consideration of interests* seems to me to involve an assertion of equality that is neither purely formal nor otiose. It *resembles,* it is true, another principle, which is deducible from the principle of formal equality—therefore itself formal—and which is often called the principle of equal consideration. The principle of formal equality states that where there

[4] [Pp. 140, 141 above.]—ED.

is no relevant difference between two cases, no rational ground exists for not treating them alike; but, conversely, where there is a relevant difference, there is a reasonable ground for treating them differently. This involves, as a corollary, that equal consideration must be given to the relevant features of each, for to have good reasons for favoring one person or course of action rather than another surely implies that there are no conclusively better reasons on the other side; and how could one know that, without having given them equal consideration?[5] This is certainly, then, a purely formal or procedural principle, for it offers no criterion for good reasons nor makes any substantive recommendation for action. The principle of equal consideration of interests, on the other hand, is specific at least to the extent that it directs consideration to the *interests* of those affected, and so lays down, as the other principle does not, a criterion of relevance. After all, if I preferred A to B because A could be of more use to me, I should still be acting consistently with the formal principle of equal consideration, provided I had first considered how useful to me B could be. But this would not be consistent with the equal consideration of interests, for I would have given thought to the interests of neither A nor B, but only to my own.

If the principle is not purely formal, neither is it otiose. For it would be perfectly possible to consider the interests of everyone affected by a decision without giving them *equal* consideration. Elitist moralities are precisely of this kind. Although the elitist would allow that ordinary men have interests deserving some consideration, the interests of the super-man, super-class, or super-race would always be preferred. Some men, it might be said, are simply worth more than others, in the sense that any claim of theirs, whatever it might be and whatever its specific ground, would always take precedence. Such a morality would maintain that there was some criterion, some qualifying condition, of race, sex, intellect, or personality, such that a person once recognized as satisfying it would automatically have prior claim in every field over others.

The egalitarian would deny that there is any such criterion.

[5] See S. I. Benn and R. S. Peters, *Social Principles and the Democratic State*, London, 1959 (reissued as *Principles of Political Thought*, New York, 1964 and 1965), Chapter V, for a fuller discussion of the formal principle of equal consideration.

Whatever priority special circumstances or properties confer on a man in particular fields, no one of them, neither a white skin, male sex, Aryan ancestry, noble birth, nor any other whatsoever, would entitle a man to move to the head of *every* queue. That is not to imply that any man can always claim the same treatment as any other, nor, indeed, that one man's interest could never have priority over another's, as, for instance, when we tax the rich to assist the poor. But every claim must be grounded on criteria specifically appropriate to it, and every demand for privilege must be argued afresh, since arguments valid in one field have no necessary consequential validity in others. This, I think, is the claim fundamental to the idea of social equality or equality of esteem. It is related to the claim to self-respect, which J. C. Davies has put in these words: "I am as good as anybody else; I may not be as clever or hard-working as you are, but I am as good as you are." [6] It bears also on the concept of equality of respect. No one could respect all men equally; nor does it seem likely, leaving aside the differences in respect we have for men on account of their different virtues and merits, that there is still a residual respect we owe to each merely as a man. What is there to respect in what alone is common to all men—membership of this particular biological species? It makes perfectly good sense, however, to say that, whereas we respect different men for different things, there is no property, such as a white skin, which is a necessary condition of a man's being worthy, whatever his other merits, of any respect at all. So every man is entitled to be taken on his own merits; there is no generally disqualifying condition.

That this is not mere empty formalism is clear when we contrast the case of men with that of animals. For not to possess human shape *is* a disqualifying condition. However faithful or intelligent a dog may be, it would be a monstrous sentimentality to attribute to him interests that could be weighed in an equal balance with those of human beings. The duties we have in respect to dogs would generally be discounted when they conflict with our duties to human beings—discounted, not set aside, for we might well decide to waive a minor obligation to a human being rather than cause intense suffering to an animal. But if the duties were at all commensurate, if, for instance, one had to de-

[6] *Human Nature in Politics,* New York, 1963, p. 45.

cide between feeding a hungry baby or a hungry dog, anyone who chose the dog would generally be reckoned morally defective, unable to recognize a fundamental inequality of claims.

This is what distinguishes our attitude to animals from our attitude to imbeciles. It would be odd to say that we ought to respect equally the dignity or personality of the imbecile and of the rational man; it is questionable indeed whether one can treat with respect someone for whom one's principal feeling is pity. But there is nothing odd about saying that we should respect their interests equally, that is, that we should give to the interests of each the same serious consideration as claims to conditions necessary for some standard of well-being that we can recognize and endorse.[7]

The imbecile has been something of an embarrassment to moral philosophers.[8] There is a traditional view, going back to the Stoics, that makes rationality the qualifying condition on which human freedom and equality depend. But if equal consideration of interests depended on rationality, imbeciles would belong to an inferior species, whose interests (if they could properly be allowed to have interests) would always have to be discounted when they competed with those of rational men. What reason could then be offered against using them like dogs or guinea pigs for, say, medical research? But, of course, we do distinguish imbeciles from animals in this regard, and although it would be quite proper to discriminate between imbeciles and rational men for very many purposes, most rationalist philosophers would concede that it would be grossly indecent to subordinate the interests of an imbecile to those of normal persons for *all* purposes, simply on the ground of his imbecility.

Nevertheless, the link between rationality and our moral concern for human interests cannot be disregarded. If the human species is more important to us than other species, with interests worthy of special consideration, each man's for his own sake, this is possibly because each of us sees in other men the image of

[7] I do not argue for this conception of interests in this paper, except by implication. I have done so explicitly, however, in "'Interests' in Politics," *Aristotelian Society Proceedings*, LX (1959–1960), pp. 123-40.

[8] For example, Bernard Williams, "I omit here, as throughout the discussion, the clinical cases of people who are mad or mentally defective, who always constitute special exceptions to what is in general true of men." "The Idea of Equality," in P. Laslett and W. G. Runciman, eds., *Philosophy, Politics and Society*, Oxford, 1962, p. 118. [Pp. 125 above.]—ED.

himself. So he recognizes in them what he knows in his own experience, the potentialities for moral freedom, for making responsible choices among ways of life open to him, for striving, no matter how mistakenly and unsuccessfully, to make of himself something worthy of his own respect. It is because this is the characteristically human enterprise, requiring a capacity for self-appraisal and criticism normal to men but not to dogs, that it seems reasonable to treat men as more important than dogs.[9]

Still, we respect the interests of men and give them priority over dogs not *insofar* as they are rational, but because rationality is the human norm. We say it is *unfair* to exploit the deficiencies of the imbecile, who falls short of the norm, just as it would be unfair, and not just ordinarily dishonest, to steal from a blind man. If we do not think in this way about dogs, it is because we do not see the irrationality of a dog as a deficiency or a handicap but as normal for the species. The characteristics, therefore, that distinguish the normal man from the normal dog make it intelligible for us to talk of other men as having interests and capacities, and therefore claims, of precisely the same kind as we make on our own behalf. But although these characteristics may provide the point of the distinction between men and other species, they are not in fact the qualifying conditions for membership, or the distinguishing criteria of the class of morally considerable persons; and this is precisely because a man does not become a member of a different species, with its own standards of normality, by reason of not possessing these characteristics. On the other hand, the deficiency is more than an accidental fact, for it has a bearing on his moral status. For if someone is deficient in this way, he is falling short of what, in some sense, he *ought* to have been, given the species to which by nature he belongs; it is, indeed, to be deprived of the possibility of fully realizing his nature. So where the mental limitations of the dog can be amusing, without lapse of taste, those of an imbecile are tragic and appalling. Moreover, so far from being a reason for disregarding his interests, they may be grounds for special compensatory consideration, to meet a special need.

[9] If we were able to establish communication with another species—dolphins, for instance—and found that they too were engaged in this "characteristically human enterprise," I think we should find ourselves thinking of them as a fishy variety of human being, making much the same claim on our consideration.

I said earlier that an egalitarian would deny that any property could confer an automatic general priority of claim on anyone possessing it, but that this need not preclude one man's interests having priority over others' in certain respects. I want to enlarge on this point and in doing so to compare the principle of equal consideration of interests with John Rawls' account of justice as fairness.[10]

Rawls asserts that "inequalities are arbitrary unless it is reasonable to expect that they will work out for everyone's advantage, and provided the positions and offices to which they attach . . . are open to all." He then seeks to show that only a practice that satisfied these conditions could be accepted by free, equal, rational, and prudent participants in it, given that they knew their own interests and that each ran the risk of filling the least favored roles. Rawls' model appears to derive justice from consent. However, what really counts is not what a man would actually accept but what, understanding his interests, he could reasonably accept. Thus objections to a practice based purely on envy of a privileged position would not be admissible, because avoiding the pangs of envy would not be an interest of a rational, prudent man. Rawls' model looks like a way of saying that a practice is just if it sacrifices no one's interest to anyone else's and makes only such distinctions as would promote the interests of everyone, given that the interests are not simply desires but conditions of well-being that rational men could endorse as such. This in turn looks rather like the egalitarian principle of equal consideration of interests. There are, however, difficulties in trying to equate the two accounts.

Rawls' model suggests an adequate schema for justifying discrimination in terms of desert or merit (the traditional problems of justice); it can be fitted, however, to modern conceptions of social justice, only at the cost of so abstracting from reality that the model loses most of its suggestiveness.[11] These conceptions are

[10] John Rawls, "Justice as Fairness," reprinted in P. Laslett and W. G. Runciman, *op. cit.*, pp. 132–57; and "Constitutional Liberty and the Concept of Justice," in Carl J. Friedrich and John W. Chapman, eds., *Justice: Nomos VI*, New York, 1963, pp. 98–125.

[11] *Cf.* John Chapman's point that, admitting the justice of Rawls' strictures on utilitarianism, the latter has this merit, as against the contractualist theories of justice, that it can take account of need. "Justice and Fairness" in *Justice, op. cit.*, pp. 147–69.

characteristically compensatory and distributive; they are implicit in the institutions and policies of welfare states, which provide for the needs of the handicapped by taxing the more fortunate. At first glance, at least, Rawls' principles of justice would give wealthy but sterile people who are taxed to help educate the children of poor but fertile people legitimate grounds for complaint, as victims of a discriminatory practice that imposes sacrifices without corresponding advantages.

It could be argued, perhaps, that Rawls meets the case by presupposing in his model that all participants start equal, and that all roles are interchangeable. The restrictions that the community's practices would put on individual interests, or the sacrifices that would be accepted by some for the benefit of others, would then be such as "a person would keep in mind if he were designing a practice in which his enemy were to assign him his place." Rawls may argue that it is always prudent for the fortunate to insure against misfortune; it would be reasonable, in that case, for a man to consent to a tax for someone else's advantage, if there were a risk of his finding himself in that person's place. But which of all the features of a man's situation, character, talents, and incapacities, by which he could be at a disadvantage, are to be taken as intrinsic and irremediable, and which conjecturally subject to reallocation, as part of the "place" to which his enemy might assign him? Need the normal, healthy person really reckon with the risk of being called upon to fill the role of the congenitally handicapped? Similar questions can be asked of some socially conferred disadvantages. While the rich must, perhaps, take account of the risk of poverty, need a white man take seriously the risk of having to fill the role of a colored man in a racially prejudiced society? To meet these arguments, Rawls would need to postulate as one of the conditions of his model, not that the participants are equal but that they are completely ignorant of all their inequalities.[12]

When pressed, then, the model becomes increasingly remote from reality. Rawls' account of justice seems to rely, at first glance, on the conception of principles to which self-interested individuals would agree; it soon becomes evident, however, that these are principles to which such individuals *could reasonably* agree. More-

[12] Or, as John Chapman has put it to me, "Rawls assumes you don't know who you are."

over, if the primary motivation of self-interest is to be preserved, we must suppose these individuals ignorant of their identities and thus unaware of any circumstances that would distinguish their own interest from anyone else's. What they are really called upon to do, then, is to safeguard a paradigmatic set of interests from a number of typical hazards. We need not now suppose a collection of egotists, so much as creatures with standards of human well-being and with both a concern for and a knowledge of the conditions necessary for achieving or maintaining it. Now the lack of some of these conditions, food and shelter for instance, would frustrate the attainment of such standards more completely than the lack of others, such as holidays or books. One must arrange human interests, then, in an order of priority, distinguishing basic from other less urgent needs. So a participant in one of Rawls' practices would be well advised to reckon with the possibility of being deprived of basic needs, as well as of being subject to a range of natural and social handicaps that would impair his capacity to supply them. Consequently, he would be rash to concur in any practice that (subject to certain provisos considered below) does not guarantee the satisfaction of basic needs and compensate for handicaps before conceding less urgent advantages to others, even if that means giving the handicapped special treatment at the expense of the normal and healthy.

Developed in this way, Rawls' model would take account of the fact that questions of social justice arise just because people are unequal in ways they can do very little to change and that only by attending to these inequalities can one be said to be giving their interests equal consideration. For their interests are not equal in the sense that every interest actually competing in a given situation is of equal weight, irrespective of how far each claimant's interests have already been attended to; they are equal, instead, in the sense that two men lacking similar conditions necessary to their well-being would, *prima facie,* have equally good claims to them.

This analysis throws some light on the paradoxical problems of compensatory welfare legislation on behalf of Negroes. A recent collection of essays[13] has drawn attention to the ambiguous implications of the notion of equality and, in particular, of the "equal

[13] R. L. Carter, D. Kenyon, Peter Marcuse, Loren Miller (with a foreword by Charles Abrams), *Equality,* New York, 1965.

protection" clause of the Fourteenth Amendment, for the desegregation and social integration of Negroes. Even liberal friends of the Negro have been known to argue, it seems, that the law should be color-blind, and that compensatory legislation on the Negro's behalf is discrimination in reverse. If (it is said) color is irrelevant to eligibility for jobs, housing, education, and social esteem, to make special provisions for the Negro as such would be to reinstate an irrelevant criterion, and so to treat equals unequally, or alternatively, to deny the human equality that it is so important to affirm. This argument disregards, however, a vital ambiguity. Negroes and whites are equal in the sense that their interests deserve equal consideration; they are painfully unequal in the sense that society imposes on the Negro special disabilities. So although black and white may equally need housing or education, the obstacles placed by society in the black man's way add extra weight to his claim to public assistance to meet these needs. Where society imposes handicaps, it can hardly be unjust for the state to compensate for them. Nor is it far-fetched to call this a way of providing equal protection for the interests of black and white. Where the interests of a group are subject to discriminatory social handicaps on the irrational ground of color, it is not irrational for the state to apply the same criterion in giving them protection on an appropriately more generous scale. Equal protection ought not to mean an equal allocation of the means of protection—for the protection must be commensurate with the threat or impediment.[14]

Finally, it is necessary to qualify the principle of equal consideration of interests in two respects, the first theoretical, the second practical.

The first corresponds to Rawls' qualification that "an inequality is allowed only if there is reason to believe that the practice with the inequality, or resulting in it, will work for the advantage of every party engaging in it." [15] The principle of equal consideration of interests provides for the satisfaction of interests in order of urgency, every individual's claim being otherwise equal. A de-

[14] G. Vlastos makes a similar point in connection with the right to security, "Justice and Equality," *Social Justice*, R. B. Brandt, ed., Englewood Cliffs, N.J.: Prentice-Hall, Inc., 1962, p. 41.

[15] "Justice as Fairness," *op. cit.*, p. 135. [Pp. 79–80 above.]—ED.

parture from this principle could be defended by showing that it would increase the capacity to satisfy interests in general and that it would not weaken the claims of someone who, without the adoption of the variant practice, could reasonably claim satisfaction under the main principle. It may be expedient, but not just, that one man should starve that others might grow fat; but there is no injustice if, in allowing some to grow fat, we can reduce the number that would otherwise starve. In this way we take account of incentive arguments for distribution by desert, as well as of claims to special treatment to meet functional needs.

The second qualification applies to the practical application of the principle. I have argued that it prescribes that interests be satisfied in order of their urgency, men without food and clothes falling further short of some presupposed conception of well-being than men who have these things but lack guitars. But clearly, this principle works as a practical guide for social policy only so long as there is a very wide measure of agreement on priorities. And there is such agreement in that range of interests we most commonly call "needs," those, in fact, from which most of my examples have been drawn. But it is not easy to see how a society that had solved the problem of providing for everyone's generally agreed needs could go much further in applying equal consideration of needs as a direct distributive principle.

Throughout this paper I have been relying on a conception of interests as conditions necessary to a way of life or to forms of activity that are endorsed as worthwhile, or (what probably amounts to the same thing) as conditions necessary to the process of making of oneself something worthy of respect.[16] Now, hermits and ascetics apart, we shall probably agree on the basic conditions necessary for any good life at all. Once given those preliminary conditions, however, we shall encounter very diverse opinions on the absolute eligibility of certain ways of life, on their relative worth, on the

[16] It is not necessary for my present purpose to discuss what could be good reasons for approving some ways of life, or forms of activity, or kinds of personality, and rejecting others. I ask the reader's assent only to the following propositions: that we do in fact make judgments of this kind, and that the notion of what is in a man's interest must ultimately be related to such a judgment, at any rate at the stage at which it is said that he is mistaking where his real interest lies. There may be sufficient consensus in a society for "interests" to function descriptively; but this is only because, at that level, the normative element is not in dispute and not therefore obtrusive.

conditions necessary for them, and on the relative urgency of such conditions, as claims to our attention. This would make it very difficult indeed to put a schedule of interests into a socially acceptable order of priority. Furthermore, it is difficult to see how an authoritative and general allocation of resources according to interests could avoid laying down an official ruling on what ways of life were most eligible. Yet, as Charles Fried has argued,[17] the freedom to judge, even mistakenly, what is in one's own interests is itself an important human interest.

This may, however, point the way out of the dilemma. My main criticism of Rawls has been that, unless amended along the lines I have indicated, his postulate of equality is either unrealistic or restrictive, removing some of the most insistent problems of social justice from the scope of his principles, by presupposing a condition that it is in the interests of justice to bring about. But in the conditions of affluence I am now considering, where basic interests are already being satisfied, and there is no further common ground on priorities, the postulate of equality would come much closer to reality. If there are equal opportunities to pursue one's interests, and freedom to determine what they are is recognized as itself an important interest, even at the risk of error, Rawls' principles of justice come into their own. Rawls lays it down that a practice is just if everyone is treated alike, unless a discrimination in favor of some is of advantage to everyone. We can now translate this into the language of equal interests: If all basic interests are already being satisfied and if there is no universally acknowledged order of priority as between further interests competing for satisfaction, then, given that the individual has a fundamental interest in determining what are his own interests, a practice would be just that gave all interests actually competing in a situation equal satisfaction, save insofar as an inequality made possible a greater degree of satisfaction without weakening claims that would be satisfied without it. On this interpretation, Rawls' original account of the criteria of a just practice turns out to be a special application, in conditions where all handicaps have already been remedied, of the principle of the equal consideration of interests.

[17] "Justice and Liberty," in *Justice, op. cit.,* pp. 126–46. See also my "'Interests' in Politics," *loc. cit.*

HUGO A. BEDAU

Radical Egalitarianism

To think as an egalitarian is to consider the degree and range of inequalities among men and to explore ways to remove or at least diminish them. Although we live in an age when egalitarianism receives a good press, we know that even today not all reflective men would regard themselves as egalitarians in the manner described above. No doubt there are reasons—some good, others not so good—for rejecting an egalitarian posture on some questions of social policy and practice. But what are those reasons, and which is which? One way to bring them under critical scrutiny is to begin by considering the idea of a radically egalitarian society. By a radically egalitarian society, I mean a society in which every other consideration yields before the demands of equality, a society in which everyone is as equal to everyone else in as many respects as is possible. Why would anyone advocate such egalitarianism? What doctrines would it embody? What principles and truths, if any, would its realization contradict?

Radical egalitarianism is the doctrine which asserts:

(1) All social inequalities are unnecessary, and unjustifiable, and ought to be eliminated.

By "social inequality" I mean not only caste, class, or other status differences but also any political, legal, or economic differences among persons, irrespective of whether the inequality results from

H. A. Bedau, "Egalitarianism and the Idea of Equality," in J. Roland Pennock and John W. Chapman, eds., *Nomos IX: Equality*, pp. 3–27 (with omissions). Reprinted in revised form by permission of the publisher, Atherton Press, Inc.

one's own choice and effort or that of another. Thus, even the differences deliberately planned as rewards or awards, or imposed as punishments, count as social inequalities. Excluded are only such inequalities as we seem to have in sex, race, color, or age, which since Rousseau have been thought of as "natural." A social inequality is something which, if others were to treat one differently, could be deliberately produced or removed (*e.g.*, differences in income, wealth, property, employment, education; and in opportunities, rights, duties, privileges). By "unjustified" I mean that the inequalities are morally indefensible not only because they may be unjust or unfair but because any of several other objections can be brought against them (*e.g.*, inutility, incompatibility with self-fulfillment). In particular this means that one finds nothing objectionable in equalities among men despite differences in needs, abilities, or merit. That you should work twice as hard as I at some common task, but in no way earn a greater reward, does not offend. That I should be a grasshopper with my life, while you, antlike, lay up for the morrow, insures only that the radical egalitarian will deny you your surplus. If he does not, he has permitted the introduction of differences of wealth, which constitute social inequalities, and these in turn will lead to other social inequalities. By "unnecessary" I mean not only that the inequalities can be diminished or eliminated but that they are not in fact a condition of anything worth preserving, and especially that the absence of such inequalities would not result in the dissolution of society or the increase in net unhappiness among men. Finally, by "eliminated" I mean deliberately diminished, through voluntary efforts or coercive action, until they vanish.

Radical egalitarianism, then, is not that "state of perfect equality" of which Locke spoke in his *Second Treatise* (§7), for as he later explains (§54), age, virtue, merit, birth, or alliances may properly give one man a "just precedency" over another without in any way interfering in their "perfect equality." Such social arrangements are clearly prohibited by (1). Karl Popper has said that "the egalitarian principle proper" is "the proposal to eliminate 'natural' privileges."[1] This is independent of radical egalitarianism, unless "natural" means "inherited," or "customary," and so forth. Ernest Barker's "Principle of Equality," namely, "Equality

[1] K. R. Popper, *The Open Society and Its Enemies* (1950), p. 94.

is . . . the beginning, not the end,"[2] is the converse of (1). Friedrich Hayek, on the other hand, in effect had (1) in mind when he attacked the principle of "complete and absolute equality of all individuals in all those points which are subject to human control,"[3] So did Isaiah Berlin, when he referred to "complete social equality," where "everything and everybody should be as similar as possible to everything and everybody else."[4] Benn and Peters, likewise, recommend only a "negative" ideal of equality and reject any "positive egalitarianism"[5] equivalent to (1). Of the writers in this volume, only J. R. Lucas, in rejecting "Equality in all respects between all men for all purposes and under all conditions," expressly confronts (1).

Radical egalitarianism is seldom formulated and rarely, if ever, discussed because its absurdities as a social ideal are too plainly apparent. How closely it approximates the aspirations of earlier utopians, anarchists, socialists, and other revolutionaries, how large an influence it exercised over their avowed doctrines and desires, are questions beyond my competence to answer. My interest here in radical egalitarianism is simply that, because it is so extreme, it may serve the purpose of organizing our thoughts on what is to be said for and against less radical and more attractive egalitarian notions.

We know, of course, that what usually goes under the name of egalitarianism is not the uncompromising and categorical demand phrased in (1), but other, humbler ideals. At the root of the desire for economic equality, for instance, lies the conviction that none should have luxuries while some lack necessities. More generally, egalitarianism consists of both a protest and a demand. As the writings of Godwin and Tawney show, the protest has always been against inequalities based on "arbitrary" or "capricious" distinctions. Consequently, the egalitarian tradition has always maintained that inequalities in class, race, religion, sex, age, wealth, and literacy (to cite only favorite candidates) do not in themselves invariably justify differences in treatment, opportunity, or rights,

[2] E. Barker, *Principles of Social and Political Theory* (1951), p. 151.

[3] F. A. Hayek, *The Road to Serfdom* (1958), p. 109.

[4] I. Berlin, "Equality," *Proceedings of the Aristotelian Society*, LVI (1956), p. 311.

[5] S. I. Benn and R. S. Peters, *The Principles of Political Thought* (1965), p. 153.

because these differences do not cancel the important similarities among men, nor are they always the source of differences that can justify inequalities (notably and usually, differences in contribution and need). The egalitarian demand (a demand made also by the libertarian) is that all, not merely a favored few, be given the opportunity for the free and unhampered development of their capacities. It is this protest against invidious distinctions and the celebration of individual self-determination that Shelley extolled in *Prometheus Unbound:*

> . . . . man
> Equal, unclassed, tribeless, and nationless,
> Exempt from awe, worship, degree, the king
> Over himself . . . .

What is the source of this protest and demand, and (for those who think the source is "the ancient vice of envy") what is its justification? It lies in four fundamental principles which are what I shall call *the principles of egalitarianism.* Although they fall well short of radical egalitarianism, they express all that one should wish to say in the name of a sound egalitarianism (and the reader will note that they are more than is allowed by the egalitarian parameters J. R. Lucas offers in his essay in this volume, the principles of "Universalisability" and "Universal Respect").

The first egalitarian principle I shall call the doctrine of *the justice of equality.* Concerning reflections on social justice, Richard Brandt has remarked recently, "The one point of agreement among contemporary thinkers seems to be that equality and justice have a close relation." [6] This close relation is not confined to the concept of *social* justice, and to my knowledge, it has never been seriously denied since Aristotle observed that "All men hold that justice is some kind of equality." (*Politics,* III. 12) Every recent attempt to analyze the concept of justice shows the acceptance of this principle. I shall phrase it this way:

(2) Justice involves equality.

This is, of course, hopelessly abstract and vague. It is important to know whether the equality here is an equality of rights (and if so, of which) or of something else; and whether treating per-

[6] R. B. Brandt, ed., *Social Justice* (1962), p. v.

sons equally, in the name of justice, involves anything more than treating them with *impartiality,* which is all that Aristotle, Hobbes, and many others have thought equality meant insofar as they thought (3) was true. I will not attempt here to summarize or improve upon the full discussion of the relation between justice and equality advanced by other writers in this volume (notably Rawls, Barry, and Benn). Unsatisfactory though (2) may be, it nevertheless puts us in mind of what accounts (perhaps entirely) for the attraction the idea of equality has for us: it is the justice of equality. If social equality has to be recommended on any moral grounds other than that of its justice, it has at best a precarious hold on our convictions. The egalitarianism of the classical utilitarians testifies to this. There is always the danger that some "recognized social expediency," in Mill's phrase, will depend upon inequality, and thus will justify overriding the equality normally required for the general happiness. If we turn to altogether nonmoral grounds in order to justify social equality, it is difficult to see how to proceed. Such aesthetic appeal as equality has occasionally had (William Dean Howells once spoke of it as "a beautiful thing, . . . the only joy, the only comfort") seems wholly consequent upon a prior recognition of its moral authority. Freed from that sanction, equality has usually been thought to have no claim on us. In More's *Utopia,* for example, we are presented with a populace whose taste is so dulled by egalitarian sympathies that each citizen is content to own but one cloak, and that one identical in cut and color with his neighbor's. It is by the aesthetics, not the morality, of such a society that we are shocked. The flatness and uniformity of an egalitarian society (required at least by the word's etymology) has always repelled all but a few. Were (2) not true, we would gladly yield to the splendors of inequality, whose "fatal beauty," as Henry Alonzo Myers noticed,[7] always exerts a powerful attraction.

The second principle I shall call *the equality of persons:*

(3) All men are equal—now and forever, in intrinsic value, inherent worth, essential nature.

For generations, it has been recognized that the doctrine of the equality of men vacillates between the apparently straight-forward

[7] H. A. Myers, *Are Men Equal?* (1955), p. 20.

empirical generalization that (a) all men *are* equal to each other, at least in some respects; the clear though contestable moral demand that (b) all men always *ought* to be treated equally, or as equals, at least in certain respects; and (3), the ancient Stoic-Christian doctrine of human equality, a proposition that is neither an empirical claim nor a moral injunction but a different sort of proposition altogether. Consider: (3) neither implies nor is implied by (a) or (b) or their conjunction; hence if (a) is false, its falsity could never be conclusive evidence against (3). On the other hand, if (a) is true, then its truth *suggests* that (3) might also be true, and conversely; if one accepts (3) then one is in a position to *protest* violations of (b). Similarly, (3) neither implies nor is implied by (1), although a radical egalitarian would almost certainly advance some version of (3) in support of (1). But a good deal more will be required to support (1); it is not owing to a lapse in logical acumen that none of the many recent philosophers who profess belief in (3) do not also embrace (1). The exact role of (3) in egalitarian thought, apart from its bearing on (2), is not to be underestimated, but I shall not attempt to add to what can be found on the subject in the previous essays in this volume by Bernard Williams and Stanley Benn.

The third principle may be called *the presumption of equality*. Again, Aristotle was the first to imply that unequal, not equal, treatment is in need of some justification, and that inequalities for which no adequate reason can be given are unjustified. Leslie Stephen phrased it more explicitly: "There should always be a sufficient reason for any difference in our treatment of our fellows." [8] If this is so, then we do not need any "sufficient reason" for treating persons equally. Hence, we may say:

> (4) Social equalities need no special justification, whereas social inequalities always do.

If there is a presumption in favor of equality, we must think it is because, *ceteris paribus*, equal treatment is the right treatment for all persons. On this understanding (4) becomes a corollary of (2), since what gives the presumption in favor of equality is the fact that justice requires it. But it is possible, as classical utilitarianism illustrates, to grant the same presumption in favor

[8] L. Stephen, "Social Equality," *Ethics* I (1891), p. 267.

of equality on the quite different ground that equality is, *ceteris paribus,* in fact a necessary condition of other social and personal goods. Likewise, if in (2), "equality" means only "impartiality," then (4) would not be a corollary of (2), because in (4) "equality" and "inequality" cannot mean "impartiality" and "partiality," respectively. I mention these points because there is some danger that (4) will not be accorded its true independence.

The presumption stated in (4), though a powerful theme in egalitarian thought, is clearly rebuttable, and it implies that the egalitarian must limit his aspirations. This need for limitation is evident in *the principle of equality* as it is likely to be formulated nowadays. It is a far cry from radical egalitarianism. In a typical recent formulation, this principle reads:

> (5) All persons are to be treated alike, except where circumstances require different treatment.[9]

There may be nothing deficient about such a view, it is not inconsistent with (2) or (3) or (4), and we know that it is an exhortation too rarely followed. But there is also nothing radical about it. It may not be in the direct line of descent from Aristotle's notion of proportionate equality, but it provides ample room to accommodate anti-egalitarian notions.

The limitations to which radical egalitarianism is subject and which issue in a principle of equality such as (5) can all be shown to derive from one or the other of two independent considerations which in effect derive from the two different senses of "require" in (5). More than half a century ago, it was alleged that biologists and anthropologists had "proved" that "progress" depends on social inequalities,[10] much as earlier economists had argued that economic progress in any society is contingent on an unequal distribution of income.[11] Today, similar views are defended not only by those who think of themselves as social or economic conservatives. They are an integral feature of every sociological theory of role-differentiation and stratification. Nor is it only economic or social *prog-*

[9] Quoted from M. Beardsley, "Equality and Obedience to Law," in S. Hook ed., *Law and Philosophy* (1964), p. 35.

[10] D. G. Ritchie, "Equality," *Contemporary Review* (1892), reprinted in his *Studies in Political and Social Ethics* (1902), p. 31.

[11] R. Lampman, "Recent Thought on Egalitarianism," *Quarterly Journal of Economics,* LXXI (1957), p. 247.

ress that is said to be contingent on inequality. "Social inequality," we are told, "is a *necessary* feature of any social system . . . it is . . . *impossible* to imagine a social system totally lacking in . . . manifestations of inequality."[12] It is not merely that highly industrialized societies are unthinkable except in terms of considerable social inequality. The implication is that every sociological model of human society—in whatever natural environment, at whatever time, and (presumably) of whatever size or duration—involves social inequalities. Even the staunchest critics of this scientific anti-egalitarianism insist only that the social inequalities necessary to social survival are far less than those which now exist or, for that matter, have existed in any known society.[13] Radical egalitarians will draw no comfort from this because it leaves untouched the major objection:

(6) Some social inequalities are necessary.

"Necessary" here means that it is in fact not possible to eliminate all inequalities, either because role-differentiation is necessary to the existence of any social system and role-stratification is equally necessary (as the cause or consequence) to role-differentiation, or for other less sophisticated reasons, for example, because some inequalities can be removed only by introducing others, or because social inequalities are an inescapable consequence of natural (individual) inequalities. As Hume long ago remarked, "Render possessions ever so equal, men's different degrees of art, care, and industry will immediately break that equality." The soundness of his point is not altered if for "possessions" we substitute "social conditions." The question that (6) raises for those with egalitarian sentiments is this: What are the minimum inequalities required to maintain a given social system and what is the cost, as measured by existing institutions that would need to be changed and by the frustration of other values, to achieve this minimum? This looks like an empirical question for some behavioral scientist to answer, and it would be interesting to know the answer for our society.

The necessary inequalities implied in (6) raise no question of

[12] W. Moore, "But Some are More Equal than Others," *American Sociological Review,* XXVIII (1963), pp. 14, 16. Italics added.

[13] See M. M. Tumin, "On Equality," *American Sociological Review,* XXVIII (1963), pp. 19–26, and further criticism at pp. 799–808.

justification. Only that which could be otherwise needs to be justified. However, if the apparent injustice of these inequalities is obviated by their social necessity, the apparent injustice of some other inequalities is negated by their moral necessity, so to speak. Certain inequalities that are avoidable or eliminable, if we may believe most philosophers, should nevertheless not only be tolerated but deliberately introduced or preserved. This is because:

(7) Some social inequalities are justifiable.

If certain inequalities are justifiable, then they are "required" in the sense of (5) no less than the inequalities in (6) are "required" because they are necessary. There is a familiar and semipopular argument to the effect that equality, whether of rights, treatment, or condition, (a) is simply incompatible with the achievement of other moral ideals, such as individual self-development and personal freedom, and that (b) there is no rational ground for a decision (whether by an individual or a government) in favor of equality and against a conflicting ideal, for example, freedom, rather than the reverse. This particular argument depends for its attractiveness in considerable part on a failure of analysis. First of all, if (b) is true, then it is difficult to see how one can accept the inference that certain inequalities are *justified.* Second, before one can conclude that (a) is true—that equality and, say, freedom are incompatible ideals—one must show that the competing ideal in question does not imply its *equal* application to all men. There undoubtedly are such ideals, but it is difficult to see how they are to survive criticism as moral ideals. This is most easily seen in the case of freedom itself. Surely, insofar as freedom is a social ideal, it is the *equal* freedom of all men that is meant. If this is conceded, then either the alleged incompatibility disappears (for equality becomes a constituent of the ideal of freedom) or else the conflict is really between (equal) freedom and some other ideal (*e.g.,* unequal power), which may or may not be a defensible ideal. Third, those who believe in the incompatibility between freedom and equality tend to think of the latter in terms of radical egalitarianism. Now, there is no doubt whatever that maximal personal freedom is incompatible with radical egalitarianism, but this hardly seems an interesting deduction; it would be distressing only if no other form or principle of egalitarianism were worth defending—which is surely not so. What holds for the relation between freedom and equality holds also, I think, for the relation between equality and every other genuine social ideal.

To turn to the arguments that philosophers have advanced on behalf of (7), they seem to be mainly of two sorts. Several generations ago David Ritchie argued that "spiritual" but not "material" inequalities among men were justified, on the ground that "spiritual inequalities are advantageous, material inequalities are not." [14] The advantages in this instance, he thought, accrued to the society as a whole. Similarly, Harold Laski argued that "it is consistent with the principle of equality that men be differently treated, so long as the differences are relevant to the common good." [15] Those who take this view follow the path marked out long ago by Bentham, the Mills, and Sidgwick, namely, that inasmuch as the net social usefulness of any mode of conduct alone justifies it as the rule, the same consideration may justify a breach of the rule; and this applies as much to maxims such as "Treat all persons equally" or "All men ought to be equal in political rights" as it does to any other moral rule. Against this, it has been argued that these purely utilitarian considerations could never demonstrate a given inequality to be a *just* inequality, even if they could demonstrate (for those prepared to accept some version of the principle of utility as their ultimate authority) a given inequality to be *justifiable*.

Other philosophers, however, have argued the more interesting position that certain inequalities are justified because they are just. Such maxims of distributive justice as "To each according to his merit," "To each according to his needs," "To each according to his work," and "To each according to his prior agreements," all appear to be anti-egalitarian maxims.[16] Yet, there seem to be many occasions where conduct is justified by appeal to these maxims in order to override criticism based on egalitarian principles. We do constantly speak of one person deserving one thing and another deserving something else; and in doing so, we often rely

[14] "Equality," p. 40. By "spiritual inequalities" Ritchie meant men's different capacities for and achievement in artistic, intellectual, and moral excellence.

[15] H. Laski, "A Plea for Equality," in his *The Dangers of Obedience* (1930), p. 232.

[16] Gregory Vlastos has argued that "To each according to his needs" is an egalitarian maxim. See his "Justice and Equality," in Brandt, ed., *Social Justice*, pp. 40 ff., 72.

on one or another of these maxims and think ourselves justified *and just* in doing so. So these inequalities are presumably thought of as just inequalities. They are inequalities, as William Frankena has put it, which are "required by *just-making* considerations (*i.e.,* by principles of *justice,* not merely *moral* principles) of substantial weight. . . ." [17] And, he adds, the practices that issue from such considerations are "not necessarily very egalitarian." A similar view has been offered by John Rawls, according to whom inequalities are just only if they work out to every person's advantage; such inequalities may be numerous and various, but they can be just and not merely justified. (Brian Barry, in section IV of his essay in this volume, criticizes Rawls' theory precisely for failing to preserve this distinction between just and justified inequalities.)

Some philosophers have even tried to argue that the principle expressed in (2) can accommodate the maxims of distributive justice without inconsistency, that is, they have offered an egalitarian defense of just inequalities. Wolfgang von Leyden has argued that treating persons unequally is justifiable only if "we must do so in order to treat them equally in another and more 'important' or more 'fundamental' respect." [18] Gregory Vlastos has gone further, insisting that inequalities (*e.g.,* an unequal distribution of some good) can be justified only if the reasons justifying them are the very reasons normally justifying equality.[19] On such views, a correct understanding of the principle of equal distribution, of recognizing persons' equal right to whatever good may be in question (freedom, security, welfare, property), in fact not only permits but requires introducing inequalities. Hence, inequalities may not only be just, they can even be justified by the principles of egalitarian justice!

The result is a conception of egalitarianism that not only is immeasurably distant from radical egalitarianism but that has also gone a long way to accommodate meritarian considerations. It has become enormously complex in theory as well. To treat people equally now involves always considering (and often trying to effect) deviations from strict equality in at least three dimen-

[17] W. K. Frankena, "The Concept of Social Justice," in Brandt, ed., *Social Justice,* p. 10. Italics in the original.

[18] W. von Leyden, "On Justifying Inequalities," *Political Studies,* XI (1963), p. 68.

[19] "Justice and Equality," pp. 39 ff.

sions simultaneously (to accommodate variations in persons' merit, work, and prior agreements). Surely the ironic consequence of such attempts to justify inequalities in the name of egalitarianism is that by all odds the strongest practical argument for egalitarianism has always been recognition of the fact that "human justice has, in many cases, to be the justice of mere equality, simply because of the difficulties of assigning proportionate equalities fairly." [20] This is not to say that giving way to "mere equality" on grounds of simplicity is to fall back upon utilitarian considerations, as is sometimes alleged. The reason that justifies distribution according to mere equality when the complexities of proportionate equality get out of hand is presumably that this is the *fairest* way to make a distribution; in effect, one has in mind (2) and (5), and *ex hypothesi* the circumstances make the "except" clause of (5) inapplicable. In such situations, it remains an open question whether the simplest pattern of distribution is the most useful; the strict egalitarian need not worry if it is the most useful *because* it is the fairest! But it is not an open question whether it is the fairest, for one is unable to carry out a properly weighted or proportionately equal distribution, that is, to identify and carry out any distribution that is *fairer*. There is not space to argue for one rather than another of these ways to defend (7). But I see no way to reject (7), whatever its proper defense may entail. The upshot for radical egalitarianism is the same in any case.

Once we isolate the principles of egalitarian thought, (2) through (5), and the limitations they must face, (6) and (7), there is not much left of (1). (6) and (7) show that (1) is false, although, of course, they do not likewise refute any or all of (2) through (5). These principles remain as the quadrants of social justice, equalitarian instruments for social criticism and reform. And instead of the extreme and somewhat frightening notion of radical egalitarianism, what we have left is:

(8) All social inequalities not necessary or justifiable should be eliminated.

This is rather tepid by comparison with (1), and taken by itself, it may not be very interesting or novel, though it is hardly a

[20] D. G. Ritchie, "Equality," p. 34; cf. L. Stephen, "Social Equality," p. 265. Recently, the same objection has been advanced to the way Rawls' theory copes with this problem; see Brian Barry, *Political Argument* (1965), pp. 321–22.

platitude. Even so it will be too radical for some, although they can take some comfort in its ample ambiguities and in the theoretically endless factual arguments it invites.

What this review of egalitarian thinking shows is that egalitarianism is incapable of resisting considerations of social necessity and of morality (including, perhaps, considerations of egalitarian justice itself) that have the effect of justifying, or at least of removing from condemnation, an enormous number and variety of social inequalities. "We have as yet no direct experience," one sociologist has recently reminded us, "of the way of life of an egalitarian society." [21] Nor are we likely to. At any given time, some inequalities are bound to be socially necessary, others morally justified, and still others naturally necessary. We are and will remain surrounded both in fact and in theory by inequalities of every sort. This may help us to understand how it is possible for so many persons to question the wisdom (and impugn the motives) of those who would condemn and undertake to eliminate a particular social inequality. For the truth of the matter is that almost every actual difference among men can be a source or basis of some justifiable inequality, if not in public life then in private, if not in large matters then in small. The permanent task for the egalitarian remains one of scrutinizing existing inequalities among men in order to assure us that they are based on justifiable (or at least unavoidable) differences, and to eliminate those which are not.[22]

[21] T. B. Bottomore, *Elites and Society* (1964), p. 140.

[22] In two recent articles criteria have been proposed to determine the egalitarianism of a given distribution. See H. R. Alker, Jr. and B. M. Russell, "On Measuring Inequality," *Behavioral Science,* IX (1964), pp. 207–18, and F. E. Oppenheim, "Egalitarianism as a Descriptive Concept," *American Philosophical Quarterly,* VII (1970), pp. 143–52.

Bibliographical Essay

A number of treatises are now available for students who wish to pursue further study of justice and equality. Among recent volumes of special value to those with philosophical interests are: OTTO A. BIRD, *The Idea of Justice* (New York: Frederick A. Praeger, 1967); GEORGIO DEL VECCHIO, *Justice—An Historical and Philosophical Essay,* ed. A. H. Campbell (Edinburgh University Press, 1956); CHAIM PERELMAN, *Justice* (New York: Random House, 1967); NICHOLAS RESCHER, *Distributive Justice* (Indianapolis: Bobbs-Merrill, 1966). All these volumes have extensive notes and bibliographies.

Many other books are also available, though not written by philosophers or for a philosophical audience. Nevertheless, they are useful for their historical, political, medical, legal, religious, and other considerations which can be a stimulus to philosophical analysis and criticism: C. K. ALLEN, *Aspects of Justice* (London: Steven and Sons, 1958); P. W. BALDWIN, *Social Justice* (Oxford: Pergamon Press, 1966); EDMUND BERGLER and JOOST A. M. MEERLOO, *Justice and Injustice* (New York: Grune and Stratton, 1963); EDGAR BODENHEIMER, *Treatise on Justice* (New York: Philosophical Library, 1967); EMIL BRUNNER, *Justice and the Social Order* (New York: Harpers, 1945); EDMOND CAHN, *The Sense of Injustice* (Bloomington: Indiana University Press, 1964); LUIGI CIVARDI, *Christianity and Social Justice* (Fresno: Academy Guild Press, 1961); MORRIS GINSBERG, *On Justice in Society* (Ithaca: Cornell University Press, 1965); HANS KELSEN, *What Is Justice?* (Berkeley and Los Angeles: University of California Press, 1957); OTTO KIRCHHEIMER, *Political Justice* (Princeton University Press, 1961); SANFORD A. LAKOFF, *Equality in Political Philosophy* (Cambridge: Harvard University Press, 1964); H. H. MARSHALL, *Natural Justice* (London: Sweet and Maxwell, 1959); W. G. RUNCIMAN, *Relative Deprivation and Social Justice* (London: Routledge, 1966); JULIUS STONE,

Human Law and Human Justice (Stanford University Press, 1965); THOMAS SZASZ, *Psychiatric Justice* (New York: Macmillan, 1965); R. H. TAWNEY, *Equality* (New York: Capricorn Books, 1952); JOHN WILSON, *Equality* (New York: Harcourt Brace Jovanovich, 1966).

In addition to the above monographs, there are several volumes containing scholarly essays on a wide variety of topics in which questions of justice and equality are paramount: RICHARD BRANDT, ed., *Social Justice* (Englewood Cliffs: Prentice-Hall, Inc., 1962); LYMAN BRYSON, ed., *Aspects of Human Equality* (New York: Harpers, 1956); CARL J. FRIEDRICH and JOHN W. CHAPMAN, eds., *Nomos VI: Justice* (New York: Atherton Press, 1963); FREDERICK A. OLAFSON, ed., *Justice and Social Policy* (Englewood Cliffs: Prentice-Hall, Inc., 1961); J. ROLAND PENNOCK and JOHN W. CHAPMAN, eds., *Nomos IX: Equality* (New York: Atherton Press, 1967).

Considerable assistance in interpreting and evaluating philosophical theories of justice and equality may be obtained by studying these views in the larger context of the history of social and political thought, or in systematic treatises in political philosophy or in ethics. Among the recent volumes in these areas which deserve mention are: GEORGE H. SABINE, *A History of Political Theory,* 3rd ed. (New York: Holt, 1961); JOHN PLAMENATZ, *Man and Society,* 2 vols. (New York: McGraw-Hill, 1963); BRIAN BARRY, *Political Argument* (New York: Humanities Press, 1965); J. R. LUCAS, *The Principles of Politics* (Oxford: Clarendon Press, 1966); STANLEY I. BENN and RICHARD H. PETERS, *The Principles of Political Thought* (New York: Macmillan, 1964); RICHARD B. BRANDT, *Ethical Theory* (Englewood Cliffs: Prentice-Hall, Inc., 1959); JOHN HOSPERS, *Human Conduct* (New York: Harcourt Brace Jovanovich, 1961).

Articles and essays too numerous to mention continue to appear in the standard scholarly (philosophical, legal, political) journals. Deserving of special mention because of their use to students are the following survey and encyclopedia articles: STANLEY I. BENN, "Moral and Social Equality," *The Encyclopedia of Philosophy,* III (1967), pp. 38–42, and "Justice," *The Encyclopedia of Philosophy,* IV (1967), pp. 298–302; FELIX E. OPPENHEIM and IRVING KRISTOL, "Equality", *International Encyclopedia of the Social Sciences,* V (1968), pp. 102–11; EDMOND CAHN, "Justice", *International Encyclopedia of the Social Sciences,* VIII (1968), pp. 341–47; ROBERT M. HUTCHINS *et al.,* eds., "The Idea of Equality", in *The Great Ideas Today: 1968* (1968), pp. 302–50.

Aristotle. The standard complete critical English text of Aristotle is the Oxford University Press edition of *The Works of Aristotle,* ed. W. D. ROSS, in twelve volumes, 1908–1952. Volume IX contains *The Nichomachean Ethics* complete. Other translations of this treatise are readily available, including those in paperback by J. A. K. THOMPSON (Penguin) and MARTIN OSTWALD (Library of Liberal Arts). The development of moral thought in ancient Greece, including a discussion of Aristotle's ethical views, can be found in the highly original monograph by A. W. H. ADKINS, *Merit and Responsibility* (Oxford University Press, 1960). The best elementary discussion of Aristotle's entire philosophy, which provides the setting of his ethical views, is the volume by W. D. ROSS, *Aristotle,* 6th ed. (London: Methuen, 1955). The most recent English commentary on *The Nichomachean Ethics* is by W. F. R. HARDIE in his *Aristotle's Ethical Theory* (Oxford: Clarendon Press, 1968). An extensive discussion of Aristotle's views on justice, to which I am indebted, will be found in Chapter X of Hardie's book. Three very different recent essays on Aristotle's theory of justice deserve notice: HANS KELSEN, "Aristotle's Doctrine of Justice," in his *What is Justice* (1957), pp. 117–36, and reprinted in JAMES J. WALSH and HENRY L. SHAPIRO, eds., *Aristotle's Ethics* (1967), pp. 102–20; RENFORD BAMBROUGH, "Aristotle on Justice," in his *New Essays on Plato and Aristotle* (1965), pp. 159–74; and KONRAD MARC-WOGAU, "Aristotle's Theory of Corrective Justice and Reciprocity," in his *Philosophical Essays* (1967), pp. 21–40.

Hobbes. There is no complete critical text of Hobbes' work; until one appears it is necessary to use the edition by SIR WILLIAM MOLESWORTH, in sixteen volumes (11 volumes in English, 5 in Latin), published in London, 1830–1845. The third English volume contains the complete text of *Leviathan.* The most widely used complete text, accompanied by a searching critical introduction, is edited by MICHAEL OAKESHOTT and published by Basil Blackwell in 1947; another complete edition readily available is published by The Clarendon Press (Oxford) and edited in 1909 by W. POGSON SMITH. The best paperback edition of the complete text, despite its tendentious introduction, has recently been prepared by C. B. MACPHERSON (Pelican Classics); a partial text, also with a valuable introductory essay and a helpful index, has been edited by JOHN PLAMENATZ (Meridian Books). Hobbes has not always been taken seriously as a natural law theorist. For representative statements of natural law moral philosophy, which uniformly ignore or deprecate Hobbes, see A. P. D'ENTREVES, *Natural Law* (London: Hutchinson's, 1951), HEINRICH A. ROMNEN, *The Natural Law* (St. Louis: B. Herder, 1947), and JOHN COGLEY, ed., *Natural Law and the Modern World* (New York: World Publishing Co., 1963). The most influential, authoritative, and original study of the political and ethical philosophy of Hobbes is HOWARD WARRENDER'S *The Political Philosophy of Thomas Hobbes* (Oxford University Press, 1957). A more recent volume on the same subject is M. M. GOLDSMITH, *Hobbes's Science of Politics* (New York: Columbia University Press, 1966). The best recent study of *Leviathan* in its entirety is F. S. MCNEILLY, *The Anatomy of Leviathan* (London: Macmillan, 1968); this volume also includes a useful annotated bibliography. Other recent books which analyze Hobbes' moral and social philosophy in connection with his metaphysics and logic include Richard Peters, *Hobbes* (Pelican Books, 1956), and J. W. N. Watkins, *Hobbes's System of Ideas* (London: Hutchinson's, 1965).

Mill. The definitive text of Mill's writings in a uniform edition is in course of publication by the University of Toronto Press, beginning in 1963. Volume X, published in 1969, contains a critical text of *Utilitarianism* and related writings, with a useful critical introduction by D. P. Dryer. The complete text of *Utilitarianism* has long been readily available, and in several paperback editions. General studies of utilitarianism (by Elie Halevy, Leslie Stephen, and John Plamenatz) and of Mill's philosophy (by Karl Britton and R. P. Anschutz, plus two recent paperback collections: James M. Smith and Ernest Sousa, eds., *Mill's Utilitarianism* (1969) and J. B. Schneewind, ed., *Mill* (1968)) may all be consulted with profit. But they offer surprisingly little of direct analysis on Mill's views on justice and equality. For a general discussion of the growth of Mill's social and political thought, see J. W. Robson, *The Improvement of Mankind* (London: Routledge and Kegan Paul, 1968). Mill's theory of justice in relation to that of other utilitarians (Hume, Bentham, James Mill, Austin and Henry Sidgwick) has been briefly sketched by the present editor in "Justice and Classical Utilitarianism," in Carl J. Friedrich and John W. Chapman, eds., *Nomos VI: Justice* (New York: Atherton Press, 1963), pp. 284–305.

Hume. There is no adequate critical and complete English edition of Hume's philosophical writings, although for most purposes the four volume edition, *The Philosophical Works of David Hume* (first published in Edinburgh in 1826) will suffice. The complete text of his *Treatise* and two *Enquiries* is found in the editions published by Oxford University Press in 1894–1896, and edited by L. A. Selby-Bigge (these volumes contain useful indexes as well). Hume's miscellaneous political and literary essays, some of which (notably, "Of the Original Contract") are of great interest to the student of Hume's moral philosophy, may be found in the paperback volume edited by C. W. Hendel, *David Hume's Political Essays* (Indianapolis: Bobbs-Merrill, 1953). A readily available abridgment from all Hume's writings designed to facilitate the study of his ethical and social thought is to be found in the paperback volume edited by Henry David Aiken, *Hume's Moral and Political Philosophy* (New York: Hafner Publishing Co., 1948).

The standard general treatises on Hume's philosophy (by Norman Kemp Smith, Charles W. Hendel, and A. H. Basson) should be consulted even though their assistance to the novice on Hume's theories of justice and equality is minimal. The recent and comprehensive volume on Hume's political and moral thought by J. B. Stewart, *The*

Moral and Political Philosophy of David Hume (New York: C
University Press, 1963) provides a discursive rather than analytic
of its subject. Among recent essays, see I. F. G. Baxter, "David Hu
Justice," *Revue internationale de philosophie,* XIII (1959), pp.
Jonathan Harrison, "Utilitarianism, Universalization, and Ou
to Be Just," *Proceedings of the Aristotelian Society* (1952–53), p
34, and reprinted in F. A. Olafson, ed., *Justice and Social Policy*
pp. 55–79; John Day, "Hume on Justice and Allegiance," *Phi*
L (1965), pp. 35–56.

Rawls. Several essays by John Rawls subsequent to the one re
here expand his theory of justice and show its application to a
of closely related issues. See: "Constitutional Liberty and the Con
Justice," in *Nomos VI: Justice* (1963), pp. 98–125; "The Sense of J
Philosophical Review, LXXII (1963), pp. 281–305; "Legal Obligat
the Duty of Fair Play," in Sidney Hook, ed., *Law and Philosophy*
pp. 3–18; "Distributive Justice," in P. Laslett and W. G. Ru
eds., *Philosophy, Politics, and Society,* 3rd Series (1967), pp. 58–8
tributive Justice: Some Addenda," *Natural Law Forum,* XIII (19
51–71; "The Justification of Civil Disobedience," in H. A. Bed
Civil Disobedience (1969), pp. 240–55.

The argument which Rawls develops in these essays has been c
by several writers, including Brian Barry, Chaim Perelman, and
Runciman, in their works previously cited; also in essays by Jo
Chapman and Charles Fried in *Nomos VI: Justice*; and in Ro
Wolff, "A Refutation of Rawls' Theorem on Justice," *Journal of*
ophy, LXIII (1966), pp. 179–90.

moral thought in ancient Greece, including a discussion of Aristotle's ethical views, can be found in the highly original monograph by A. W. H. ADKINS, *Merit and Responsibility* (Oxford University Press, 1960). The best elementary discussion of Aristotle's entire philosophy, which provides the setting of his ethical views, is the volume by W. D. ROSS, *Aristotle,* 6th ed. (London: Methuen, 1955). The most recent English commentary on *The Nichomachean Ethics* is by W. F. R. HARDIE in his *Aristotle's Ethical Theory* (Oxford: Clarendon Press, 1968). An extensive discussion of Aristotle's views on justice, to which I am indebted, will be found in Chapter X of Hardie's book. Three very different recent essays on Aristotle's theory of justice deserve notice: HANS KELSEN, "Aristotle's Doctrine of Justice," in his *What is Justice* (1957), pp. 117–36, and reprinted in JAMES J. WALSH and HENRY L. SHAPIRO, eds., *Aristotle's Ethics* (1967), pp. 102–20; RENFORD BAMBROUGH, "Aristotle on Justice," in his *New Essays on Plato and Aristotle* (1965), pp. 159–74; and KONRAD MARC-WOGAU, "Aristotle's Theory of Corrective Justice and Reciprocity," in his *Philosophical Essays* (1967), pp. 21–40.

Hobbes. There is no complete critical text of Hobbes' work; until one appears it is necessary to use the edition by SIR WILLIAM MOLESWORTH, in sixteen volumes (11 volumes in English, 5 in Latin), published in London, 1830–1845. The third English volume contains the complete text of *Leviathan.* The most widely used complete text, accompanied by a searching critical introduction, is edited by MICHAEL OAKESHOTT and published by Basil Blackwell in 1947; another complete edition readily available is published by The Clarendon Press (Oxford) and edited in 1909 by W. POGSON SMITH. The best paperback edition of the complete text, despite its tendentious introduction, has recently been prepared by C. B. MACPHERSON (Pelican Classics); a partial text, also with a valuable introductory essay and a helpful index, has been edited by JOHN PLAMENATZ (Meridian Books). Hobbes has not always been taken seriously as a natural law theorist. For representative statements of natural law moral philosophy, which uniformly ignore or deprecate Hobbes, see A. P. D'ENTREVES, *Natural Law* (London: Hutchinson's, 1951), HEINRICH A. ROMNEN, *The Natural Law* (St. Louis: B. Herder, 1947), and JOHN COGLEY, ed., *Natural Law and the Modern World* (New York: World Publishing Co., 1963). The most influential, authoritative, and original study of the political and ethical philosophy of Hobbes is HOWARD WARRENDER's *The Political Philosophy of Thomas Hobbes* (Oxford University Press, 1957). A more recent volume on the same subject is M. M. GOLDSMITH, *Hobbes's Science of Politics* (New York: Columbia University Press, 1966). The best recent study of *Leviathan* in its entirety is F. S. MCNEILLY, *The Anatomy of Leviathan* (London: Macmillan, 1968); this volume also includes a useful annotated bibliography. Other recent books which analyze Hobbes' moral and social philosophy in connection with his metaphysics and logic include RICHARD PETERS, *Hobbes* (Pelican Books, 1956), and J. W. N. WATKINS, *Hobbes's System of Ideas* (London: Hutchinson's, 1965).

Mill. The definitive text of Mill's writings in a uniform edition is in course of publication by the University of Toronto Press, beginning in 1963. Volume X, published in 1969, contains a critical text of *Utilitarianism* and related writings, with a useful critical introduction by D. P. DRYER. The complete text of *Utilitarianism* has long been readily available, and in several paperback editions. General studies of utilitarianism (by ELIE HALEVY, LESLIE STEPHEN, and JOHN PLAMENATZ) and of Mill's philosophy (by KARL BRITTON and R. P. ANSCHUTZ, plus two recent paperback collections: JAMES M. SMITH and ERNEST SOUSA, eds., *Mill's Utilitarianism* (1969) and J. B. SCHNEEWIND, ed., *Mill* (1968)) may all be consulted with profit. But they offer surprisingly little of direct analysis on Mill's views on justice and equality. For a general discussion of the growth of Mill's social and political thought, see J. W. ROBSON, *The Improvement of Mankind* (London: Routledge and Kegan Paul, 1968). Mill's theory of justice in relation to that of other utilitarians (Hume, Bentham, James Mill, Austin and Henry Sidgwick) has been briefly sketched by the present editor in "Justice and Classical Utilitarianism," in CARL J. FRIEDRICH and JOHN W. CHAPMAN, eds., *Nomos VI: Justice* (New York: Atherton Press, 1963), pp. 284–305.

Hume. There is no adequate critical and complete English edition of Hume's philosophical writings, although for most purposes the four volume edition, *The Philosophical Works of David Hume* (first published in Edinburgh in 1826) will suffice. The complete text of his *Treatise* and two *Enquiries* is found in the editions published by Oxford University Press in 1894–1896, and edited by L. A. SELBY-BIGGE (these volumes contain useful indexes as well). Hume's miscellaneous political and literary essays, some of which (notably, "Of the Original Contract") are of great interest to the student of Hume's moral philosophy, may be found in the paperback volume edited by C. W. HENDEL, *David Hume's Political Essays* (Indianapolis: Bobbs-Merrill, 1953). A readily available abridgment from all Hume's writings designed to facilitate the study of his ethical and social thought is to be found in the paperback volume edited by HENRY DAVID AIKEN, *Hume's Moral and Political Philosophy* (New York: Hafner Publishing Co., 1948).

The standard general treatises on Hume's philosophy (by NORMAN KEMP SMITH, CHARLES W. HENDEL, and A. H. BASSON) should be consulted even though their assistance to the novice on Hume's theories of justice and equality is minimal. The recent and comprehensive volume on Hume's political and moral thought by J. B. STEWART, *The*

Moral and Political Philosophy of David Hume (New York: Columbia University Press, 1963) provides a discursive rather than analytic account of its subject. Among recent essays, see I. F. G. BAXTER, "David Hume and Justice," *Revue internationale de philosophie,* XIII (1959), pp. 112–31; JONATHAN HARRISON, "Utilitarianism, Universalization, and Our Duty to Be Just," *Proceedings of the Aristotelian Society* (1952–53), pp. 105–34, and reprinted in F. A. OLAFSON, ed., *Justice and Social Policy* (1961), pp. 55–79; JOHN DAY, "Hume on Justice and Allegiance," *Philosophy,* L (1965), pp. 35–56.

Rawls. Several essays by John Rawls subsequent to the one reprinted here expand his theory of justice and show its application to a variety of closely related issues. See: "Constitutional Liberty and the Concept of Justice," in *Nomos VI: Justice* (1963), pp. 98–125; "The Sense of Justice," *Philosophical Review,* LXXII (1963), pp. 281–305; "Legal Obligation and the Duty of Fair Play," in SIDNEY HOOK, ed., *Law and Philosophy* (1964), pp. 3–18; "Distributive Justice," in P. LASLETT and W. G. RUNCIMAN, eds., *Philosophy, Politics, and Society,* 3rd Series (1967), pp. 58–82; "Distributive Justice: Some Addenda," *Natural Law Forum,* XIII (1968), pp. 51–71; "The Justification of Civil Disobedience," in H. A. BEDAU, ed., *Civil Disobedience* (1969), pp. 240–55.

The argument which Rawls develops in these essays has been criticized by several writers, including Brian Barry, Chaim Perelman, and W. G. Runciman, in their works previously cited; also in essays by JOHN W. CHAPMAN and CHARLES FRIED in *Nomos VI: Justice*; and in ROBERT P. WOLFF, "A Refutation of Rawls' Theorem on Justice," *Journal of Philosophy,* LXIII (1966), pp. 179–90.